Favourite Recipes

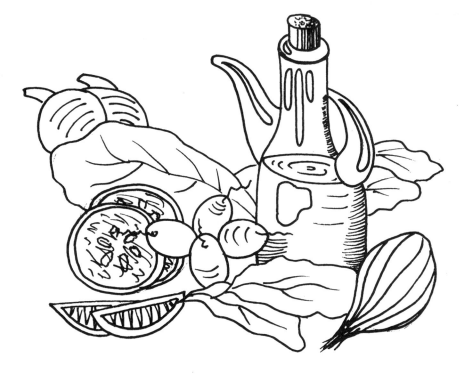

Produced by
The Women's Foreign Missionary Association
of the Free Church of Scotland

Cover Photograph by George T. Thomson, LRPS.

Design and Print by Campsie Litho Limited
Published by Campsie Marketing
51 French Street, Glasgow G40 4EH
Tel: 0141-554 5225

ISBN No. 0 9525856 0 X

Contents

Jesus said,

"I am the bread of life.
He who comes to me will never go hungry,
and he who believes in me will never be thirsty."

John Chapter 6 verse 35

Foreword

This collection of *Favourite Recipes* has been produced by the Women's Foreign Missionary Association to raise money for the Disaster and Relief Fund of the Free Church of Scotland. This fund is used to help those in our world whose lives have been affected by famine, war or other tragedy.

The W.F.M.A. want to thank most sincerely all those who have worked together in the preparation of the book.

- The friends who so generously loaned the necessary finance.

- The ladies in each congregation who collected the recipes.

- The ladies who acted as presbytery co-ordinators, making the initial selections, and those who helped with the distribution.

- The editing committee who gave up many Saturdays to select and edit the recipes.

- Those who helped to prepare the copy for the printers, particularly Anne Thomson and Anne McDonald.

- All those who were involved in the proof reading.

- George Thomson who provided the photograph for the front cover and Sheona Macdonald who helped with the composition of the picture.

- Janet Fraser who used her skills as illustrator.

- Sandra, Mark and Graeme of Campsie Litho Ltd. for their work, advice and patience!

Without the recipes there would have been no book, so a special thank you to everyone who sent in a recipe. These came from Free Church congregations throughout Scotland and in London and also from friends in associated churches in Northern Ireland, Canada, Australia, South Africa and Peru. It was unfortunate that, because of limited space, so very many good ones had to be omitted. We did try to include at least one from every congregation that participated.

Finally our thanks to all of you who have bought the book. We hope that you will enjoy using it and that some of the recipes will become your favourites too.

We rarely use a recipe book to cook a meal for ourselves. We turn to it when we want to show our love and care for our family and friends by preparing something special for them. So too, this collection of *Favourite Recipes* is an expression of our love and concern for others whose daily lives are so different from our own. It is our prayer that the money raised by its sale will, in some small way, help to alleviate their suffering and hardship and that they will discover for themselves that only Jesus is able to meet their every need and give them eternal life.

Olwen Ford
President

Oven Temperatures

Heat of Oven	Thermostat Setting	Temp in °C (approx)	Temp in °F (approx)
Very cool	1/4	110	225
	1/2	130	250
	1	140	275
Cool	2	150	300
Warm	3	170	325
Moderate	4	180	350
Fairly hot	5	190	375
	6	200	400
Hot	7	220	425
Very hot	8	230	450
	9	240	475

Starters

Minty Melon Starter

1 ripe Ogen melon, halved and flesh scooped out in balls (or cut in $^1/2$" cubes)
2 small oranges, peeled and segmented
grated rind and juice of 1 lime
$^1/2$ oz (15g) blanched almonds, toasted
2 tblsp fresh mint, chopped
small lettuce, washed and shredded
few sprigs mint to garnish

Method:

1 Place melon and oranges in bowl.
2 Mix together lime juice, nuts and mint.
3 Pour over fruit and leave to stand for 30 minutes.
4 Divide into 4 and serve on bed of lettuce.
5 Garnish with mint.

I. Sutherland, Lairg

Prawn and Melon Cocktail

4 tblsp salad cream
1-2 tblsp tomato sauce to taste
1 sml carton double cream, beaten thick
$^1/2$ tblsp lemon juice

$^1/2$-1 melon, scooped into balls
sml/med bag frozen prawns, defrosted
1 lemon, cut in wedges
lettuce, shredded
paprika

Method:

1 Mix salad cream and tomato sauce in bowl, fold in cream and juice.
2 Gently mix in melon balls and prawns ensuring they are well coated in creamy sauce.
3 Serve on a bed of shredded lettuce with a wedge of lemon.
4 Sprinkle with paprika before serving.

Annabel Robertson, Dundee

 *Starters*

Avocado with Prawns

1 ripe avocado
1 tblsp lemon juice
3-4 oz (75-100g) large prawns
lettuce leaves

3 tblsp fromage frais
2 tblsp thick cut marmalade,
   warmed slightly

Method:

1 Peel avocado, remove stone, slice lengthways and pull apart to create a fan.
2 Brush with lemon juice and arrange with prawns on a bed of lettuce leaves.
3 Mix fromage frais with marmalade and serve with the avocado and prawns.

Ina Macleod, Kyle

Garlic Mushrooms

2 doz mushrooms, peeled
4 oz (100g) butter
salt and pepper
2 cloves of garlic, crushed

juice of $^1/_2$ lemon
1 tblsp parsley
1 tsp vinegar
pinch sugar
watercress

Method

1 Heat all ingredients (except mushrooms) in butter.
2 Simmer gently for 2 minutes.
3 Remove stems from mushrooms, place in oven dish, pour mixture
   over mushrooms and replace stems.
4 Cook in pre-heated oven at 220°C/425°F/Gas 7 until tender.
5 Serve 6 per person in sweetcorn dishes.
6 Garnish with watercress.

Neen Macdonald, Callanish, Lewis

Ceviche

1 lb (450g) haddock or other firm-fleshed
fish, boned and cut in $^1/_2$" (5mm) cubes
1 small green pimento, finely chopped
1 small green chilli, finely chopped
handful fresh parsley, finely chopped

1 onion, chopped
juice of 2 limes (or lemons)
1 tblsp olive oil
salt

Method:

1 Mix all the ingredients well together and put them in a covered bowl in the refrigerator
   overnight.
2 Eat it raw. It is "cooked" by action of juices.
   (Note: The fish must be very fresh.)

Julia Smith, Lima, Peru

Crab Pancakes

4 oz (100g) white crab meat   a little milk
1 tblsp S.R. flour   salt and pepper
1 egg   1 tblsp oil

Method:

1 Mix all ingredients together (except oil).
2 Add a little milk if mixture is too stiff.
3 Fry spoonfuls of mixture in oil until golden and crispy.
   (Note: Grated cheese and onion can be added to mixture if desired.)

Anne Mackinnon, North Uist and Grimsay

Smoked Salmon Crisps

4 large slices bread   4-6 oz (100-175g) smoked salmon
2 tblsp milk beaten with 1 egg   juice of $^1/_2$ lemon
2 tblsp corn oil   watercress
1 oz (25g) butter

Method:

1 Remove crusts from bread and trim each slice into a neat square.
2 Soak in egg and milk mixture.
3 Put butter and oil in frying pan and stand over medium heat.
4 When it is hot and sizzling, reduce heat to low and add bread slices.
5 Fry until crisp and brown, drain on kitchen paper.
6 Transfer to 4 serving plates, cover with salmon, sprinkle with lemon juice and garnish
   with watercress. Serve while bread is still warm.

C. Mackenzie, Saltcoats

Pan Fried Scallops

1 lb (450g) fresh scallops   salt
   (3 or 4 per person)   garlic pepper
1 egg, beaten   lettuce, shredded
breadcrumbs   lemon to garnish

Method:

1 Dip fresh scallops in beaten egg then toss in breadcrumbs.
2 Fry scallops in hot melted butter.
3 Sprinkle with salt and garlic pepper.
4 Serve in large scallop shell on bed of lettuce and garnish with lemon wedges.

Joan Morrison, North Uist and Grimsay

 *Starters*

Salmon Mousse

4 1/2 fl oz (125ml) hot water
1 chicken stock cube
1 tblsp gelatine
8 oz (225g) tin of salmon and juice
2 tblsp mayonnaise or salad cream

1 carton (125g) plain yoghurt
  (or cream)
2 tsp lemon juice (or vinegar)
1/2 small onion, chopped
salt and pepper

Method:

1 Dissolve stock cube and gelatine in water.
2 Blend all ingredients together and pour into moulds to set.
3 Turn out and decorate as required.

Ella Macdonald, Duirinish, Skye

Lobster Paté

4 oz (100g) butter
2 tblsp mayonnaise
3 tblsp cream cheese

8 oz (225g) lobster meat, chopped
salt and pepper
cayenne pepper

Method:

1 Put butter, mayonnaise and cheese into a food processor and mix well.
2 Add lobster and season to taste.
3 Chill and serve with toast.

J. Mackenzie, Kinloch, Lewis

Sardine and Mushroom Paté

Equal amounts of:-
mushrooms
sardines
Philadelphia Cheese

2 oz (50g) butter, melted
juice of 2 lemons
salt to taste
black pepper

Method:

1 Sauté the mushrooms in butter, remove from heat and leave to cool.
2 Put mushrooms, sardines and Philadelphia Cheese into a liquidiser and blend
    until smooth.
3 Add lemon juice, salt and pepper and mix well.
4 Press into a mould and leave in fridge until set.
5 Garnish with a sliced mushroom and serve with crackers.

Morna Macleod, Sleat Sunday School, Skye

Smoked Mackerel Paté

12 oz (350g) smoked mackerel
8 oz (225g) butter, melted
$^1/_2$ pt (300ml) cream (or $^1/_4$ pt cream and $^1/_4$ pt natural yoghurt)
juice of 1 lemon
salt and pepper

Method:

1   Skin and bone mackerel.
2   Put melted butter and fish in liquidiser and process.
3   Add other ingredients and liquidise briefly.
4   Pour into dish and chill.
5   Serve with toast.
    (Note: A teaspoon horseradish sauce may be added if desired.)

Margaret Cope, Fortrose

Chopped Liver (Jewish)

1 lb (450g) liver (chicken is best
   but any other will do)
a little oil
2 onions, chopped

2 hard boiled eggs, chopped
2 cloves garlic, crushed
salt and pepper
paprika

Method:

1   Fry livers with one of the onions in oil until tender.
2   Mix with rest of ingredients in blender.
3   Serve on buttered toast or biscuits.

Moshe Radcliffe, Shettleston, Glasgow

Soups

Lentil and Bacon Broth

1 oz (25g) lard
8 oz (225g) lentils, soaked and drained
3 oz (75g) smoked bacon, chopped
8 oz (225g) onions, chopped
8 oz (225g) carrots, sliced
6 oz (175g) celery, chopped

1 ^{1}/$_2$ pts (900ml) chicken stock
pinch of nutmeg
1 bay leaf
^{1}/$_2$ tsp dried thyme
salt and pepper

Method:

1   Melt lard, add bacon and vegetables and fry for 5 minutes.
2   Add lentils, stir in stock, nutmeg, bay leaf, thyme and seasoning.
3   Bring to boil and simmer for 45 minutes to 1 hour.
4   Remove bay leaf and purée.

C. Murray, Back, Lewis

Curried Lentil Soup

1 onion, finely chopped
1 carrot, finely chopped
1 celery stalk, finely chopped
2 tblsp sunflower oil
1 tblsp curry paste

6 oz (175g) red lentils, rinsed
1^1/$_2$ pts (900ml) vegetable/ham stock
1 oz (25g) creamed coconut
salt and pepper

Method:

1   Fry all vegetables in oil in a large pan over low heat for 5 minutes.
2   Stir in curry paste and fry briefly.
3   Add lentils and stock and bring gently to the boil.
4   Reduce heat and simmer for 45 minutes.
5   Stir in creamed coconut and season. Purée if desired.

Sadie MacLean, St Vincent St. - Milton, Glasgow

Scotch Broth

2 oz (50g) barley
1 oz (25g) dried peas
4 pts (2 litres) cold water
4 oz (100g) turnip, diced
6 oz (175g) carrot, diced

1 onion, diced
8 oz mutton or beef
1 leek, sliced
$^1/_4$ small cabbage, finely shredded
chopped parsley

Method:

1 Put barley and peas in cold water, bring to the boil.
2 Add diced vegetables, cook slowly for 1 hour.
3 Add meat and continue cooking for another $1^1/_2$-2 hours.
4 Add cabbage and leek 20 minutes before serving.
5 Garnish with parsley

Mary Rosie, Wick

Black Isle Tattie Soup

1 oz (25g) butter/fat
2 lb (900g) potatoes, diced
1 large onion, chopped
2 celery stalks, chopped
2 pts (1 litre) beef stock

salt and pepper
10 fl oz (300ml) milk
1 tblsp flour
chopped parsley

Method:

1 Fry vegetables in melted butter in a large pan for about 10 minutes.
2 Add stock, salt and pepper.
3 Liquidise or mash with potato masher.
4 Blend flour with milk and add to soup to thicken.
5 Garnish with parsley before serving.

A. Holm, Ferintosh

Tomato Soup

1 oz (25g) butter
1 large onion, chopped
1 medium carrot, chopped
1 small celery stalk, chopped
1 lb (450g) ripe tomatoes or 14 oz (400g) tin
1 $^1/_2$ pts (900ml) chicken or vegetable stock

2 tblsp tomato puree
1 tsp sugar
$^1/_4$ tsp dried marjoram
salt
freshly ground black pepper

Method:

1 Melt butter, add onion, carrot and celery, fry until soft.
2 Add all remaining ingredients and bring to the boil.
3 Season to taste, cover pan and simmer until carrot is soft.
4 Cool slightly and liquidise.

Elizabeth MacLeod, Elder Memorial, Leith

 *Soups*

Mushroom Soup

2 oz (50g) butter	10 fl oz (300ml) milk
8 oz (225g) mushrooms, sliced	1 tblsp flour
10 fl oz (300ml) chicken stock	salt and pepper

Method:

1 Melt ³/₄ of butter in pan, add mushrooms and fry for 3 minutes.
2 Pour in stock and milk, bring to the boil then simmer, covered, for 20 minutes.
3 Purée in liquidiser.
4 Melt remaining butter in rinsed out pan, stir in flour to form smooth paste.
5 Gradually stir into puréed soup and bring back to the boil.
6 Season to taste.

Joan Boyd, North Uist and Grimsay

Carrot and Courgette Soup

1 lb (450g) carrots, chopped	2 tsp tomato purée
1 lb (450g) courgettes, sliced	2 pts (1 litre) water
2 bay leaves	2 chicken stock cubes
2 tsp sugar	salt and pepper

Method:

1 Put all ingredients into pan and boil for about 30 minutes.
2 Cool, remove bay leaves, liquidise and season to taste.

Donna MacIver, East Kilbride

Curried Carrot Soup

1 oz (25g) margarine	1 tsp sugar
1 small onion, finely chopped	juice ¹/₂ lemon
1 lb (450g) carrots, roughly chopped	salt, freshly ground black pepper
2 tsp mild curry powder	¹/₂ pt single cream
1 pt (600ml) vegetable stock	1 tblsp finely chopped parsley

Method:

1 Melt margarine, add carrots and onion.
2 Cover and cook over gentle heat for 5 minutes.
3 Stir in curry powder then pour in stock.
4 Add sugar, lemon juice and season to taste.
5 Cover and simmer over low heat for about 10 minutes until carrots are soft.
6 Leave to cool then purée in blender.
7 Return to pan and heat thoroughly.
8 Swirl cream into each portion and sprinkle with parsley.
   (Note: Turnip, pumpkin or parsnip may be used as variations.) *Mairi MacDonald, Cumbernauld*

Leek and Almond Soup

1 oz (25g) butter/margarine
2 medium onions, finely chopped
1 medium potato, diced
5 medium leeks, thinly sliced
1 small dessert apple, diced

2 pts (1 litre) chicken stock
salt and black pepper
2 oz (50g) ground almonds
1/2 pt (300ml) single cream
toasted flaked almonds to garnish

Method:

1 Heat butter, cook onions gently for 5 minutes.
2 Stir in potato, leeks, apple and cook for further 4 minutes.
3 Pour in stock and seasoning, bring to the boil.
4 Lower heat, simmer for 25 minutes.
5 Cool and liquidise or sieve (can be frozen at this stage).
6 Blend together ground almonds and cream, whisk into soup.
7 Heat, add seasoning to taste.
8 Sprinkle flaked toasted almonds on top of each serving.

Maureen Murray, Rogart

Courgette and Ginger Soup

1 lb (450g) courgettes (or marrow), sliced
2 carrots, chopped
1 small onion, chopped
1 small turnip, chopped
1 1/2 oz (40g) butter

2 pts (1 litre) chicken stock
salt and pepper
1 tsp ground ginger or to taste
5 fl oz (75ml) cream
bread croutons for garnish

Method:

1 Fry vegetables in butter until soft but not brown.
2 Add stock and seasoning, simmer for 30 minutes.
3 Blend the soup, add more seasoning if required and ginger to taste.
4 Add cream and serve soup with croutons.

Christine Campbell, Lochgilphead

Quick Asparagus Soup

1 10 oz (275g) tin asparagus spears
1 tub low fat Cheddarie cheese
4 oz (100g) potatoes, cooked
1 tblsp lemon juice

1/4 pt (150ml) milk
3/4 pt (425ml) chicken stock
salt and pepper
swirl of cream and chives to garnish

Method:

1 Put asparagus in blender with potatoes, cheese, milk and lemon juice.
2 Put in pan, add stock and heat gently and thoroughly.
3 Season and garnish.

Marion Morrison, St Vincent St. - Milton, Glasgow

 *Soups*

Celery Soup

7 oz (200g) celery, roughly chopped
1 small potato, cut in large cubes
1 small leek, cut in rings
cold water

1 ¹/₂ oz (40g) butter
1 ³/₄ pts (1025ml) stock
salt to taste

Method:

1 Soak leeks in water for 10 minutes.
2 Melt butter in pan, add vegetables, cover and sweat gently for 5 minutes stirring occasionally to make sure vegetables do not stick.
3 Add stock and salt, boil gently for 20 minutes until vegetables are soft.
4 Blend the mixture thoroughly.   *Catherine Mackenzie, Assynt*

Broccoli Soup

1 tblsp sunflower oil
6 oz (175g) peeled potato, chopped
1 medium onion, chopped
1 lb (450g) broccoli

1 ¹/₂ pts (900ml) chicken stock
¹/₂ tsp sugar
6 oz (175g) mature cheddar cheese, grated
salt and pepper

Method:

1 Fry onion and potato gently in oil.
2 Cut broccoli stems in ¹/₂" (5mm) slices, add to pan, fry for 5 minutes and season.
3 Reserve some broccoli florets and add remainder to potato mixture.
4 Add stock, simmer for 20 minutes until vegetables are soft.
5 Add remaining broccoli and sugar and blend. Most of mixture will be smooth but newly added broccoli will give grainy texture.
6 Pour into tureen, season, and stir in cheese until melted.
   (Note: Single cream added instead of cheese gives a pleasant flavour.) *M. Macarthur, Dornoch*

Cucumber Soup

knob of butter
1 cucumber, sliced
2 shallots
2 tblsp rice

salt and pepper to taste
2 pts (1 litre) chicken stock
2 tblsp cream
2 egg yolks

Method:

1 Sauté cucumber and shallots in butter.
2 Add rice and cook until rice is soft.
3 Add stock, season, bring to the boil, then simmer for 10 minutes
4 Remove from heat, liquidize, return to pan and heat to near boiling.
5 Put egg yolks and cream in warmed soup tureen, beat together.
6 Pour hot soup into tureen and serve.   *J. Everitt, Dornoch*

Creamy Corn Chowder

2 oz (50g) butter
1 small onion, chopped
2 celery stalks, chopped
2 oz (50g) plain flour
2 pts (1 litre) milk

1 chicken stock cube
11 oz (300g) tin sweetcorn
$^1/_4$ pint (150ml) single cream
4 oz (100g) cottage cheese
chopped parsley to garnish

Method:

1 Melt butter, sauté onion and celery until soft.
2 Add flour, gradually stir in milk, and add chicken stock cube.
3 Cook and stir over a medium heat until mixture begins to boil.
4 Add corn, cream and cottage cheese.
5 Reheat, but do not boil.
6 Garnish with chopped parsley.

Janet Murchison, Buccleuch & Greyfriars, Edinburgh

Cullen Skink

8 oz (225g) potatoes, diced
1 large onion, chopped
$^3/_4$ pt (425ml) milk

1 lb (450g) smoked haddock
1 oz (25g) butter
salt and pepper

Method:

1 Put potatoes, onion and milk in pan, cook until vegetables are soft.
2 Cut fish into chunks, add, cover and simmer for 20 minutes until cooked.
3 Stir in butter and season just before serving.

Ann Gillies, Dunblane

Fish Soup

1 medium or small haddock/whiting
   with bone in
1 pt (600ml) lightly salted water
1 medium onion, finely chopped
2 medium potatoes, diced
1 level tsp oatmeal

knob of butter
1 pt (600ml) milk
salt and pepper
chopped parsley and
chives

Method:

1 Simmer fish in water until flesh starts to come away from bone.
2 Strain liquid, add onion, potatoes, oatmeal, butter and cook until potatoes are soft.
3 Flake fish, carefully removing every bone.
4 Add fish and milk, season to taste, bring slowly to boil.
5 Serve with chopped parsley and chives.

Margaret Main, Burghead

 *Soups*

Atlantic Fish Chowder

$1^1/_2$ lbs (675g) fresh or frozen seafood
eg. shrimps, mussels, fish fillets of any kind
2 tblsp margarine
2 cups onion, thinly sliced
1 cup celery slices
1 cup hot water

2 cups raw potatoes, diced
1 cup carrot slices
1 tsp salt
2 cups milk
$^1/_2$ cup cheddar cheese, grated

Method:

1 Sauté onion and celery slices in margarine in large saucepan.
2 Add water, potatoes, carrots and salt, bring to boil and simmer for 10 minutes.
3 Cut fish into bite size pieces and add to the vegetables, cover and simmer for 10 minutes longer.
4 Add milk and cheese, heat over low/medium heat stirring gently until cheese melts. DO NOT BOIL. Season to taste.

K. Macaskill, Carloway, Lewis

Cheese Soup

2 oz (50g) butter
1 small onion, finely chopped
$1^1/_2$ oz (40g) flour
1 pt (600ml) milk
2 tsp salt, pinch pepper

1 pt (600ml) stock
3 small carrots, finely chopped
2 celery stalks, finely chopped
8 oz (225g) cheddar cheese, grated
parsley to garnish

Method:

1 Fry onion in butter until tender.
2 Add flour and cook slowly for 1 minute stirring well.
3 Add milk and stock, stirring continuously and bring to boil.
4 Add carrots, celery and seasoning and cook until tender.
5 Stir in cheese and heat gently until melted.
6 Garnish with parsley before serving.

Rachel Macdonald, Kilmorack

Oatmeal Soup

knob of butter
1 large onion, chopped
1 med carrot, chopped
1 med piece turnip, chopped
2 leeks, chopped

2 oz (50g) oatmeal
$1^1/_2$ pts (900ml) stock
salt and pepper
1 pt (600ml) milk

Method:

1 Melt butter in pan, add vegetables and toss until clear, cover pan with lid and cook for 5 minutes.
2 Stir in oatmeal and cook for a further 5 minutes.
3 Add stock, turn down heat, simmer for 50 minutes.
4 Add seasoning and just before serving, add milk and reheat.

Dolina Macleod, Cross, Lewis

Salads

Cucumber Salad

1 lime table jelly
$^1/_2$ pt (300ml) water
5 oz (150g) hazelnut yoghurt
2 tblsp mayonnaise

1 dsp lemon juice
1 tblsp onion, grated
2 oz (50g) cucumber, grated

Method:

1 Melt jelly in water and leave until almost set.
2 Whisk in yoghurt and mayonnaise.
3 Add lemon juice, onion and cucumber.
4 Turn into mould and chill until set.

Elizabeth Woosley, Crumlin E. P. C., N. Ireland

Salad Delight

15 oz (425g) tin crushed pineapple
1 lemon or lime jelly
8 fl oz (300ml) boiling water

1 tblsp salad cream
1 carton cottage cheese
2 carrots, grated
2 sticks celery, chopped
8 fl oz (300ml) whipping cream

Method:

1 Drain juice from pineapple.
2 Dissolve jelly in boiling water and leave until partially set.
3 Add salad cream, cottage cheese, carrots, celery and pineapple.
4 Whip cream stiffly and add to mixture.
5 Pour into mould and allow to set.

Anne MacIver, St. Vincent St. - Milton, Glasgow

 *Salad*

Blackcurrant and Beetroot Jelly

1 blackcurrant jelly
$^1/_4$ pt (150ml) water
$^1/_4$ pt (150ml) beetroot juice
1 small jar baby beets, sliced

Method:

1   Melt jelly in water and add beetroot juice.
2   Put sliced beetroot into bowl and pour in jelly,
3   Leave to set in refrigerator.
    (Variations: Carrot in orange jelly, grapes in lime jelly, cucumber in lemon jelly.
                Adjust water to requirements.)

Agnes Morrison, Shawbost, Lewis

Country Cottage Platter

1 small iceberg lettuce
12 oz (350g) cottage cheese with pineapple
4 oz (100g) honey roast ham, chopped
4 fresh nectarines, sliced
4 oz (100g) grapes, halved and de-seeded

Method:

1   Arrange lettuce on serving dish.
2   Mix cottage cheese and ham and place in centre of lettuce.
3   Arrange nectarine slices and grapes on top.
4   Serve with wholemeal French stick.

I. Sutherland, Lairg

Salad Surprise

7 oz (200g) tin cooked ham, chopped
3 oz (75g) cheddar cheese, cubed
4 oz (100g) dried apricots, chopped
4 oz (100g) sultanas
salad dressing as required

2 bananas, sliced
2 apples, sliced
2 pears, sliced
2 kiwi fruit, sliced

Method:

1   Mix all ingredients with salad dressing.
2   Serve with hot garlic bread.

Irene Howat, Campbeltown

Mexican Salad

1 lettuce, chopped
1 small can sweetcorn
1 small can kidney beans

$^1/_2$ red pepper, chopped
$^1/_2$ green pepper, chopped
$^1/_4$ cucumber, sliced
2 tomatoes, sliced

Method:

1 Arrange lettuce on serving dish.
2 Add drained sweetcorn and kidney beans.
3 Sprinkle peppers on top.
4 Arrange cucumber and tomato slices around dish.
5 Serve with salad dressing.

Margaret MacLeod, St. Columba's, Edinburgh

South African Rice Salad

Salad:

3 cups cooked rice
3 cups peaches, diced
1 onion, chopped
1 stick celery, chopped
1 green pepper, chopped
$^1/_4$ cup walnuts
$^1/_4$ cup raisins

Sauce:

$^1/_4$ cup cooking oil
2 tblsp vinegar
2 tblsp chutney
2 tblsp soya sauce
1 tsp curry powder
salt and pepper to taste

Method:

1 Mix salad ingredients.
2 Mix sauce ingredients and add to salad ingredients.
   (Note: Keeps for two days in refrigerator)

Marion Fraser, Cape Town, South Africa

Vegetarian

Potato Latkes

2 lb (900g) potatoes, grated and drained
1 onion, grated
1 egg, beaten
1 tblsp S. R. flour
oil as required
salt and pepper to taste

Method:

1 Mix ingredients (except oil) together.
2 Heat oil in frying pan.
3 Drop tablespoons of mixture into pan.
4 Fry on both sides until brown.
5 Drain well and serve.
   (Note: The secret of successful latkes is to drain the potatoes well. For best results use a
      muslin bag.)

Nellie McCabe, C.W.I., Glasgow

Cheesey Garlic Potatoes

2 lb (900g) potatoes, thinly sliced
4 oz (100g) Swiss gruyère cheese,
   grated
1 or 2 cloves garlic, crushed

salt and pepper
2 oz (50g) butter
1/2 pt (300ml) milk

Method:

1 Rinse potatoes well in water.
2 Mix cheese and garlic.
3 Layer potato slices and cheese mixture in a shallow, greased baking dish, sprinkling each
   layer with seasoning and dots of butter.
4 Heat milk to boiling point and pour into dish down the sides.
5 Cook in a pre-heated oven 200°C/400°F/Gas 6 for 45-55 minutes until the top is well
   browned.
   (Note: Cheddar cheese may also be used to make this tasty snack meal.)

Jacqui Allan, Glen Urquhart

Skirlie

3 oz (75g) suet

6 oz (175g) oatmeal

1 onion, chopped

salt and pepper

Method:

1 Melt suet in frying pan and fry onion for 2 minutes.
2 Add oatmeal and seasoning and cook on a fairly high heat.
3 Stir until oatmeal is browned.
4 Serve immediately.

Dolina MacLeod, Cross, Lewis

Pakoras

$^1/2$ cup gram flour

$^1/2$ tsp ground red chillies

water

$^1/2$ tsp cumin powder

spinach

$^1/2$ tsp turmeric powder

salt to taste

fat for deep frying

Method:

1 Make a batter of the flour and water, then add spices.
2 Cut spinach leaves in small pieces.
3 Dip in batter and deep fry in hot fat.
   (Note: Instead of spinach, cauliflower florets, pieces of potato, onion or cooked chicken may be used.)

Alina McKenzie, Service to Overseas Students, Glasgow

Guacamole (Mexican for Avocado)

1 packet Tacos

1 small tin kidney beans

1 onion, chopped

1 avocado

1 tblsp oil

$^1/2$ tsp lemon juice

1 tsp cumin powder

1 iceberg lettuce

1 clove garlic, crushed (optional)

3 oz (75g) cheese, grated

1 tblsp tomato ketchup

Method:

1 Warm Tacos in oven.
2 Fry half onion in oil and add cumin, garlic and ketchup.
3 Add drained beans to mixture and keep hot.
4 Peel avocado and purée flesh, then add remaining onion and lemon juice.
5 Put some avocado mixture in shells, then top with bean mixture.
6 Place on bed of shredded lettuce and sprinkle cheese on top.

Esther Ramirez, Lima, Peru

Cheese Fritters

1 egg, separated

4 oz (100g) plain flour

4 oz (100g) cheese, grated

pinch of salt

pinch of dry mustard

oil for frying

Method:

1   Beat white of egg until stiff.
2   Mix flour, cheese, salt and mustard with egg yolk and a little water.
3   Fold beaten egg white into mixture.
4   Drop dessertspoons of mixture into hot oil.
5   Fry until crispy, drain and serve hot.

Anne Thomson, Drumchapel, Glasgow

Campaigner Night Risotto

1   Cook 4 oz (100g) of long grain rice.
2   Prepare a selection of "extras".
    e.g. - sliced onions, peppers, celery, leeks, mushrooms, drained olives, carrot sticks or any other vegetables.
3   Sauté the firmer vegetables first in hot oil in a large pan, adding the softer ones later.
4   Small pieces of meat, chicken, "pepperami" or fish may also be added.
5   Lastly stir in the cooked rice and heat thoroughly.
6   Season well and add a squeeze of lemon juice.

Dumfries Congregation

Savoury Rice (Indian)

2 cups long grain rice

2 tblsp oil or ghee

1 1/2 medium onions, finely sliced

1 stick cinnamon

4 cardamum pods

4 whole cloves

3 1/2 cups chicken stock

1/2 cup carrot, grated

2 tsp salt

Method:

1   Wash rice well in several changes of water.
2   Heat oil in saucepan and fry onions, cinnamon, cardamum and cloves until onions are golden brown. Stir frequently to get even brown colour.
3   Add rice and fry for about 3 minutes, pour on stock and stir in grated carrot.
4   Add salt, stir in carefully and bring quickly back to boil.
5   Cover with tight-fitting lid and turn heat down to low. Leave for 20 minutes without removing lid.
6   Lift lid, allow steam to escape, pick out whole spices and fluff up lightly with a fork.
7   Turn out on to a serving dish and garnish.

Joan MacDonald, Bishopbriggs

Vegetable Curry

2 tblsp vegetable oil
2 onions, chopped
4 garlic cloves, chopped
2 carrots, chopped
2 potatoes, chopped
1 red and 1 green pepper, chopped
2 courgettes, sliced
1 pt (600ml) water
1/2 medium cauliflower, florets
4 tblsp desiccated coconut
1 tblsp lemon juice
4 tomatoes, chopped
4 fl oz (100ml) natural yoghurt

1 tsp of:-
ground ginger
cayenne pepper
cinnamon
turmeric
cumin

2 tsp of:-
ground coriander
poppy seeds

Method:

1   Heat oil in deep saucepan, add onions and garlic and cook gently until soft.
2   Add all the spices and poppy seeds, stirring well and cook for 2-3 minutes.
3   Add vegetables (except cauliflower) to pan.
4   Pour in water and stir well to combine all ingredients.
5   Bring slowly to the boil and simmer for 15-20 minutes.
6   Add cauliflower, coconut and lemon juice and cook for a further 5 minutes.
7   Add tomatoes, stir in yoghurt and simmer for 5 more minutes.
8   Serve with brown rice, salad and wholemeal bread.
    (Note: Be careful not to overcook the vegetables. This dish is best left overnight to
        allow the spices and vegetables to blend.)   *Jessie MacKinnon, Greenock*

Nut Roast

1 tblsp oil
2 onions, chopped
1 green pepper, chopped
3 oz (75g) breadcrumbs
3 oz (75g) Brazil nuts
3 oz (75g) hazelnuts
2 oz (50g) walnuts

1 garlic clove, chopped
1 tsp mixed herbs
1 tsp curry powder
8 oz (225g) tomatoes, chopped
salt and pepper
1 egg beaten

Method:

1   Fry onion and pepper in oil until soft.
2   Mix breadcrumbs, nuts, garlic, herbs and curry powder in bowl.
3   Stir in onion, pepper, tomatoes and seasoning.
4   Mix together and bind with beaten egg.
5   Put in a greased 2 lb loaf tin.
6   Bake in a pre-heated oven 220°C/425°F/Gas 7 for 30-40 minutes.
7   Serve with a green salad, rice, etc.   *Mairi Ferguson, Aultbea*

Mushroom Roast

1 oz (25g) butter
1 large onion, chopped
1 green pepper, chopped
4 oz (100g) mushrooms, sliced

4 oz (100g) breadcrumbs
3 eggs, beaten
4 oz (100g) cheese, grated
pinch of mixed herbs

Method:

1   Melt butter in pan, gently fry onion, pepper and mushrooms.
2   Cook for 2 minutes and remove from heat.
3   Add breadcrumbs and eggs to mixture.
4   Press into a greased loaf tin and cover with cheese and herbs.
5   Bake in a pre-heated oven 180°C/350°F/Gas 4 for 45 minutes.
6   Serve with tomato sauce.

Sauce:

Mix together and simmer for 15 minutes –

5 oz (150g) tin concentrated tomato purée
1 pt (600ml) water
2 tsp sugar, 1 tsp salt, 1 bay leaf

N. Scott, Kirkcaldy

Cheese and Nut Loaf

4 oz (100g) butter
4 oz (100g) S. R. flour
4 oz (100g) wholemeal flour
4 oz (100g) wholemeal breadcrumbs
4 oz (100g) mixed nuts
6 oz (175g) cheddar cheese, grated
1 tsp mixed herbs
salt and pepper

4 oz (100g) onions, finely chopped
2 eggs, beaten
1/4 pt (150ml) milk

Method:

1   Rub butter into flours to resemble fine breadcrumbs.
2   Add breadcrumbs, nuts, cheese, herbs and seasoning and mix well.
3   Sauté onions in 1/2 oz butter and add to dry ingredients.
4   Add eggs and sufficient milk to bind ingredients together.
5   Pour mixture into a lightly greased 2 lb loaf tin.
6   Cover with foil and bake in a pre-heated oven 180°C/350°F/Gas 4 for 1 1/2 hours.
7   Remove foil and bake for a further 15 minutes.
8   Cool in tin and serve sliced with a green salad.

Cathie MacLeod, Glen Urquhart

Courgette Gratin

2 tblsp oil	1 oz (25g) margarine
2 onions, chopped	1 oz (25g) wholemeal flour
1 clove garlic, chopped	$^1/_2$ pt (300ml) milk
12 oz (350g) courgettes, sliced	4 oz (100g) cheese, grated
1 tblsp parsley, chopped	1 tblsp wholewheat breadcrumbs
1 tblsp thyme, chopped	
salt and pepper	
4 tomatoes, peeled and sliced	

Method:

1 Heat oil in pan, cook onions until soft.
2 Stir in garlic, courgettes, herbs and seasoning.
3 Put half of mixture into an ovenproof dish.
4 Spread with layer of tomatoes, then spoon remaining mixture on top.
5 Melt margarine in pan, add flour and cook for 2 minutes.
6 Add milk gradually, bring to boil and stir to make sauce.
7 Add half of cheese to sauce and pour over vegetable mix.
8 Sprinkle with remaining cheese and breadcrumbs.
9 Cook in a pre-heated oven 180°C/350°F/Gas 4 for 30 minutes.   *K. Fraser, Sleat, Skye*

Vegetable Crumble

8 oz (225g) cauliflower florets	$1^1/_2$ oz (40g) margarine
8 oz (225g) broccoli florets	$1^1/_2$ oz (40g) plain flour
2 oz (50g) frozen peas	$^3/_4$ pt (425ml) milk
1 red pepper, diced	2 tsp French mustard
1 leek, chopped	salt and pepper

Method:

1 Boil cauliflower and broccoli for 5 minutes.
2 Add peas, pepper and leek and boil for a further 4 minutes, then drain well.
3 Melt margarine, add flour and cook for 2 minutes.
4 Gradually add milk, bring to boil, stirring to make sauce.
5 Season sauce, add mustard and fold in vegetables.
6 Pour into an ovenproof dish and cover with crumble.
7 Cook in a pre-heated oven 190°C/375°F/Gas 5 for 15-20 minutes.

Crumble:

3 oz (75g) brown breadcrumbs	3 oz (75g) margarine
3 oz (75g) oatflakes	3 oz (75g) cheddar cheese, grated

1 Mix breadcrumbs and oatflakes and rub in margarine.
2 Stir in cheese and use mixture to cover vegetables.   *Morag Moir, Fortrose*

Cauliflower Crunch

1 large cauliflower, cooked
2 oz (50g) butter
1 onion, sliced
4 oz (100g) mushrooms, sliced
1 oz (25g) plain flour
^{1}/4 pt (150ml) milk

5 oz (150g) natural yoghurt
salt and pepper
4 oz (100g) cheese, grated
2 hard boiled eggs
1 oz (25g) breadcrumbs

Method:

1 Divide cauliflower into pieces and place in an ovenproof dish.
2 Sauté onions and mushrooms in 1 oz butter for 2 minutes.
3 Add mixture to cauliflower.
4 Melt remaining butter, add flour and cook for 2 minutes.
5 Gradually add the milk, bring to boil, stirring to make sauce
6 Blend in yoghurt, seasoning and half the cheese.
7 Chop eggs, place on vegetable mixture and cover with sauce.
8 Sprinkle with remaining cheese and breadcrumbs.
9 Cook in a pre-heated oven 180°C/350°F/Gas 4 for 15 minutes.

Ann Gillies, Dunblane

Lentil and Vegetable Hotpot

2 tblsp oil
1 onion, sliced
1 clove garlic, crushed
2 carrots, sliced
6 oz (175g) red lentils, rinsed
1 cooking apple, diced
1 pt (600ml) water

12 oz (350g) cauliflower florets
6 oz (175g) mushrooms, sliced
2 medium courgettes, sliced
14 oz (400g) tin tomatoes, chopped
3 tblsp tomato purée
1 tblsp parsley, chopped
^{1}/2 pt (300ml) vegetable stock
2-3 potatoes, sliced

Method:

1 Heat oil in pan, fry onion and garlic until soft.
2 Add carrots, lentils, apple and cook for 2-3 minutes.
3 Add water, bring to boil and simmer for approx. 20 minutes until lentils are tender.
4 Stir in cauliflower, mushrooms, courgettes, tomatoes, purée, parsley and stock.
5 Spoon mixture into an ovenproof dish.
6 Shallow fry potatoes in oil for 5 minutes and drain.
7 Arrange on top of lentil mixture.
8 Cook in a pre-heated oven 200°C/400°F/Gas 6 for 30 minutes.
9 Garnish with parsley and serve.

K. Fraser, Sleat, Skye

Fish

Sole Confetti

2 sole fillets
1 tomato, skinned,
    deseeded and chopped
1 shallot, chopped
2 mushrooms, chopped

1 tblsp dried tarragon
1 sherry glass of white wine
salt
freshly ground black pepper
3 tblsp single cream
parsley, chopped for garnish

Method:

1 Roll fillets and place in an ovenproof dish.
2 Spread over all other ingredients (except cream and parsley).
3 Cover with foil.
4 Cook in a pre-heated oven 180°C/350°F/Gas 4 for 10 minutes.
5 Remove fish carefully and place on heated serving dish.
6 Add cream to other ingredients and heat through.
7 Spoon over fish and garnish with parsley.

Mary Ann Stewart, Dumbarton

Moray Fish Fillets

1-2 lb fish fillets (smoked or white fish may be used)
12 oz (350g) long grain rice, cooked
12 oz (350g) onion, chopped
1 oz (25g) butter
1 ¹/₂ oz (40g) flour
1 pt (600ml) milk

8 oz (225g) cheese, grated
2 tsp curry powder
salt and pepper
1 tblsp lemon juice

Method:

1 Grease an ovenproof dish and cover base with rice.
2 Sauté onions in melted butter.
3 Add flour and milk and cook, stirring until thickened.
4 Add cheese, curry powder and seasoning.
5 Place fish on rice, sprinkle with lemon juice and cover with cheese sauce.
6 Cook in a pre-heated oven 180°C/350°F/Gas 4 for 40 minutes.
7 Serve on a bed of rice.

R. Gall, Burghead

 *Fish*

Yoghurt Baked Fish

4 haddock fillets
$^1/_2$ pt (300ml) natural yoghurt
1 tblsp lemon juice
2 tblsp parsley, chopped
salt and pepper

2 oz (50g) cheese, grated
4 oz (100g) breadcrumbs

Method:

1 Wash and dry fillets and place in ovenproof dish.
2 Mix together yoghurt, lemon juice, parsley and seasoning and spoon over fish.
3 Mix together the cheese and breadcrumbs and sprinkle on top.
4 Cook in a pre-heated oven 200°C/400°F/Gas 6 for 20-25 minutes.

J. Johnstone, Paisley

Herbie Haddock

4 haddock fillets
1 oz (25g) margarine
2 oz (50g) brown breadcrumbs
4 oz (100g) cheese, grated

1 tsp mixed herbs
1 tblsp parsley, chopped
salt and pepper
$^1/_4$ pt (140ml) milk

Method:

1 Wash fish and place in ovenproof dish.
2 Melt margarine and add breadcrumbs, cheese, herbs, parsley and seasoning.
3 Mix together and spread over fish.
4 Pour milk **around** fish.
5 Cook in a pre-heated oven 190°C/375°F/Gas 5 for 15 minutes.

Isobel Smith, Ayr

Quick Fish (Microwaved)

8 oz (225g) whiting
salt and pepper
2 tblsp salad cream
sprig of parsley

Method:

1 Place seasoned fish in dish of appropriate size.
2 Cover fish thickly with salad cream.
3 Microwave on "Full Power" for 4 minutes.
4 Garnish with parsley and serve.

Chris MacKay, Govanhill, Glasgow

Cod with Orange Sauce

4 cod cutlets, well seasoned
1 oz (25g) butter
1 oz (25g) white breadcrumbs
1 oz (25g) cheese, grated

3 small oranges, peeled and thinly sliced
1 tblsp oil
1 tblsp lemon juice
1 bunch watercress

Method:

1   Dot fish with half the butter and grill for 5 minutes.
2   Mix breadcrumbs and cheese together.
3   Turn cutlets, cover with cheese mixture, dot with remaining butter and grill for a further 5 minutes.
4   Meanwhile mix orange slices with oil and lemon juice.
5   Place cutlets on long serving dish.
6   Drain oranges, arrange around fish and garnish with watercress.   *Margaret Ann Nicolson, Lochs, Lewis*

Thatched Cod

4 pieces cod (or haddock)
1 ^{1}/2 oz (40g) butter
4 oz (100g) onion, chopped
2 oz (50g) white breadcrumbs
2 oz (50g) cheese, grated

3 tomatoes, skinned and chopped
1 tsp parsley, chopped
1 lemon, grated rind and juice
salt and pepper

Method:

1   Melt ^{1}/2 oz butter and use a little to grease the base of an ovenproof dish.
2   Arrange fillets in a single layer and brush with remaining melted butter.
3   Fry onion in 1 oz butter and add breadcrumbs, cheese, tomatoes, parsley, lemon rind and juice and seasoning.
4   Spoon mixture over fillets.
5   Cook in a pre-heated oven 190°C/375°F/Gas 5 for 30-40 minutes.   *Jess Skinner, Stornoway, Lewis*

Stuffed Sole

8 small or 6 medium fillets of sole

Filling:

^{1}/2 cup breadcrumbs
4 oz (100g) cheese, grated

2 oz (50g) margarine
1 small onion, grated

Method:

1   Mix all filling ingredients together.
2   Place 4 (or 3) fillets in buttered casserole, cover with filling, lay remaining fillets on top and dot with butter.
3   Cook in a pre-heated oven 160°C/325°F/Gas 3 for 30-40 minutes.

K. N. MacDonald, Stornoway, Lewis

 *Fish*

Special Fish Pie

1 lb (450g) haddock (mixed, smoked and plain)
1 1/2 oz (40g) flour
2 oz (50g) butter   1 onion, finely chopped
3/4 pt (425ml) milk   4 oz (100g) prawns
1/2 tsp mustard powder   salt and pepper
6 oz (175g) cheese, grated

Method:

1   Dip fish in a little flour and lay half in an ovenproof dish.
2   Melt butter, stir in flour, gradually stir in milk and cook gently until thickened.
3   Add mustard powder, 4 oz cheese and seasoning.
4   Stir until cheese is melted and then add onions and prawns.
5   Pour half the sauce over the fish in dish.
6   Place remainder of fish on top and cover with rest of sauce.
7   Sprinkle remaining cheese on top.
8   Cook in a pre-heated oven 160°C/325°F/Gas 3 for 40 minutes.
9   Serve on a bed of rice.

Christine MacDonald, Dunblane

Russian Fish Pie

6 oz (175g) puff pastry   **White Sauce:**
8 oz (225g) cooked fish   1 oz (25g) flour
1 hard boiled egg, chopped   1 oz (25g) butter
1/2 tsp parsley, chopped   1/2 pt (300ml) milk
grated lemon rind
salt and cayenne pepper

Method:

1   Roll pastry into square.
2   Flake fish, add egg, parsley, lemon rind and seasoning.
3   Combine fish mixture with 1/4 pt of white sauce.
4   Put filling on pastry, fold corners to centre and seal.
5   Brush with beaten egg or milk to glaze.
6   Cook in a pre-heated oven 230°C/450°F/Gas 8 for 30 minutes.

J. MacClure, Sleat, Skye

Plain Baked Herring

1   Clean, scale and wash herrings.
2   Cut off tails and heads.
3   Put the fish into a greased ovenproof dish.
4   Brush with melted margarine, sprinkle with salt and pepper.
5   Cook in a pre-heated oven 160°C/325°F/Gas 3 for 20-30 minutes.
    (If preferred bone and roll herring before baking.)

Catherine MacIver, Point, Lewis

Soused Herring or Mackerel

6 herring or mackerel
salt and pepper
2 cloves

2 bay leaves
$^1/_8$ pt (75ml) vinegar
$^1/_4$ pt (150ml) water

Method:

1 Wash and trim fish. (If herring are used they must be boned).
2 Roll up and place in pie dish.
3 Add seasoning, cloves and bay leaves and cover with vinegar and water.
4 Cook in a pre-heated oven 190°C/375°F/Gas 5 for 45 minutes.

Margaret MacLeod, Knock, Lewis

Garlic Mackerel

6 large or 8 small mackerel fillets
1 clove garlic
1 egg, beaten
seasoned flour

butter for frying
lemon juice

Method:

1 Mince garlic finely, divide between fillets and rub in well.
2 Dip mackerel in beaten egg and then coat in flour.
3 Fry in butter for 4-5 minutes on each side.
4 Sprinkle with lemon juice and serve.

P. MacLeod, Borve, Lewis

Cockles in Butter

1 Wash cockles thoroughly and put in a large pan without water and heat until shells open.
2 Shell cockles and when cold toss in melted butter to which garlic and/or 1 dsp of sherry may be added if desired.
3 Serve with green salad and/or tartare sauce.

Catherine MacKay, Scalpay, Harris

Clam Omelette

3 eggs, beaten
$^1/_2$-1 cup milk
salt and pepper
5 or 6 clams, shelled and chopped

fish dressing
2 tomatoes, sliced
butter for cooking

Method:

1 Add milk and seasoning to beaten eggs.
2 Heat a little butter in frying pan and pour in mixture.
3 Cook until base is quite firm, then add chopped clams.
4 Sprinkle with fish dressing and decorate with sliced tomatoes.
5 Finish off cooking under grill until medium brown and risen.

C. MacSween, Scalpay Harris

 *Fish*

Stuffed Trout

6-8 trout (remove head, fins and back-bone)
4 oz (100g) onion, roughly chopped
3 tblsp oil
$^1/_2$ oz (15g) fresh root ginger, peeled and chopped
1 lb (450g) ripe dessert pears, peeled and chopped
3 oz coarse oatmeal
1 tsp vinegar
salt and pepper
2 tsp ginger wine
3 tblsp water
chopped parsley

Method:

1 Sauté onion in oil until soft, then add ginger, pears and oatmeal to pan and stir on low
   heat for 1 minute.
2 Add vinegar and seasoning and leave to cool.
3 Divide pear mixture between fish, folding each one over stuffing.
4 Place in ovenproof dish, pour over ginger wine with 3 tblsp water and cover with foil.
5 Cook in pre-heated oven 200°C/400°F/Gas 6 for 25-30 minutes.
6 Serve garnished with parsley.

Chrissie Ann MacLeod, Lochs, Lewis

Tuna and Cucumber Flan

8" shortcrust pastry flan
7 $^1/_2$ oz (220g) tin tuna fish
2" piece cucumber, chopped
4 tblsp mayonnaise

2 level tsp gelatine
2 tblsp cider or wine vinegar
2 tblsp water
salt and pepper

Method:

1 Drain and flake tuna.
2 Add cucumber and mayonnaise.
3 Dissolve gelatine in water and vinegar and add to mixture.
4 Season mixture and spoon into baked flan case.
5 Chill and decorate as desired.

Marion Morrison, St. Vincent St.-Milton, Glasgow

Meat & Poultry

Marinated Beef Steak

4 slices beef steak
1-2 tsp double cream
4 tblsp oil
2 tblsp red wine vinegar
4-5 dashes tabasco

1 tsp mustard
2 onions, chopped
2 tblsp tomato ketchup
1 clove garlic, chopped
1 tblsp Worcester sauce

Method:

1   Make marinade by mixing everything except the steak and the cream.
2   Soak the steak in the marinade for 1 hour.
3   Grill the meat, turning and basting over with the marinade for 6-8 minutes.
4   Heat marinade, add cream and serve over meat.

Donna Janssens, Urray

Gingered Beef

$1^1/2$ lbs braising steak, cubed
2 oz (50g) plain flour
salt and pepper
$1^1/2$-2 tsp ground ginger
3 tblsp oil
1 tblsp root ginger, grated
1 clove garlic, chopped

2 onions, sliced
$1/2$ pt (300ml) beef stock
8 oz (225g) tin tomatoes
2 tblsp vinegar
1 tblsp Worcester sauce
1 tblsp thick honey
15 oz (425g) tin red kidney beans, drained

Method:

1   Coat the meat with flour, seasoning and ground ginger.
2   Fry the meat in oil until brown and put in casserole.
3   Fry root ginger, garlic and onion in oil until light brown.
4   Gradually add stock, tomatoes, vinegar, Worcester sauce, honey and seasoning.
5   Bring to boil, pour into casserole over meat and put on lid.
6   Cook in a pre-heated oven 160°C/325F/Gas 3 for $1^3/4$ hours.
7   Add red beans, stir and adjust seasoning.
8   Replace lid and return to oven for 20-25 minutes.

Christine Morrison, Bon Accord, Aberdeen

Californian Beef Casserole

1 1/2 lb stewing steak, cubed
1 oz (25g) flour
1 oz (25g) fat
1 onion, sliced
1 beef stock cube
1/2 pt (300ml) hot water
1/4 pt (150ml) red wine

4-6 prunes
2 oz (50g) raisins
4 oz (100g) button mushrooms
salt and pepper

Method:

1 Coat the meat in seasoned flour.
2 Heat fat in heavy saucepan, brown meat and add onion.
3 Dissolve stock cube in water and add to meat.
4 Add wine, stir well and bring to the boil.
5 Add prunes and raisins and put into covered casserole.
6 Cook in a pre-heated oven 150°C/300°F/Gas 2 for 1¼ hours.
7 Add mushrooms and continue to cook for a further 45 minutes or until meat is tender.
   (Note: Don't be put off by the unusual ingredients - this is a delicious dish.)

Ena Smith, Free North, Inverness

Braised Steak

1 1/2 lb sirloin steak
1 tblsp cooking oil
1 onion, chopped
1 clove garlic, chopped
salt and freshly ground black pepper

1 glass red wine
1 bay leaf
1 red pepper, chopped
1 tsp cornflour

Method:

1 Fry onion in oil until soft, add garlic and ground pepper.
2 Increase heat and fry steak to seal on both sides.
3 Add wine, bay leaf and red pepper.
4 Simmer for 30 minutes and add salt to taste.
5 Remove steaks and keep warm.
6 Thicken juices with cornflour and pour over steaks.

Brenda MacFarlane, Lochs, Lewis

Beef Mexicana

¹/2 lb (225g) stewing steak, cubed
1 dsp flour
salt and pepper
1 dsp cooking oil
2 oz (50g) mushrooms, sliced
5 oz (150g) tin of tomatoes

1 tblsp black cherry jam
1 tblsp honey
1 tblsp mustard
¹/2 beef stock cube
8 fl oz (240ml) water

Method:

1 Coat the meat in seasoned flour.
2 Heat oil in saucepan, brown meat and transfer into casserole.
3 Add mushrooms, tomatoes, jam, honey and mustard.
4 Dissolve stock cube in water and add sufficient to casserole to cover meat and
    vegetables.
5 Cook in a pre-heated oven 160°C/325°F/Gas 3 for 2 hours.

Marina MacKenzie, Cole Abbey, London

Curried Beef Olives

2 tblsp cooking oil
1 large onion, grated
1 apple, chopped
1 tsp curry powder
3 oz (75g) breadcrumbs
1 tblsp sultanas
1 tblsp coconut
1 tblsp chutney

6 thin slices rump steak
2 tblsp plain flour
salt and pepper
³/4 pt (425ml) beef stock

Method:

1 Lightly fry the onion and apple in 1 tblsp oil, add curry powder and stir in breadcrumbs,
    sultanas, coconut and chutney.
2 Divide the mixture into 6 portions.
3 Season slices of steak and put a portion of filling on each slice.
4 Roll up securely and coat in seasoned flour.
5 Brown the olives in 1 tblsp oil, add stock to pan and simmer for 1¹/2 - 2 hours.
    (Alternatively, cook in a covered casserole in a pre-heated oven 150°C/300F/Gas 2 for
    1 ¹/2-2 hours.)

Sadie MacLean, St. Vincent St.-Milton, Glasgow

Mam's Dutch Roast

1 lb (450g) steak mince
1 cup breadcrumbs
1 dsp tomato ketchup
1 egg
³/4 tsp mixed herbs
1 dash Worcester sauce
salt and pepper

2 onions, quartered
2 carrots, cubed
2 parsnips, cubed
4-6 tblsp cooking oil
Topping (optional):
2 tblsp tomato ketchup
2 tblsp demerara sugar

Method:

1 Mix the mince, breadcrumbs, ketchup, egg, herbs, sauce and seasoning.
2 Shape mixture into a roll and put in a roasting tin.
3 Place vegetables around.
4 Heat oil and pour over meat and vegetables.
5 Roast in a pre-heated oven 190°C/375°F/Gas 5 for 1-1¹/2 hours.
6 Baste frequently or cover with foil, removing the foil for the last 20 minutes.
7 Coat with topping of mixed ketchup and demerara sugar.
8 Serve with the gravy and roast or creamed potatoes.
   (Variations: 1 Make mince mixture into beefburgers.
             2 Make mince mixture into balls and serve with tomato sauce and rice.)

Cora MacKenzie, Coatbridge

Chilli con Carne

1 lb (450g) steak mince
2 tblsp cooking oil
1 large onion
1 clove garlic, finely chopped
2-3 tsp chilli powder
14 oz (400g) tin tomatoes
1 tsp sugar
2 tblsp tomato purée

1 green pepper, deseeded
   and sliced
¹/4 pt (150ml) beef stock
1 tblsp lemon juice
¹/2 tsp salt
black pepper
15 oz (450g) tin red kidney
   beans, drained

Method:

1 Heat oil and fry onion with the garlic until clear.
2 Add mince and chilli powder, stirring until brown.
3 Stir in tomatoes, sugar, tomato purée, green pepper, stock, lemon juice and seasoning.
4 Bring to the boil, lower heat, cover and simmer for 30 minutes.
5 Add beans and cook for 5 more minutes.

Rae MacKinnon, Grant St., Glasgow

Hungarian Goulash

beef dripping or oil
12 oz (350g) red onions, chopped
1 tblsp paprika
2 1/4 lb (1000g) stewing steak, cubed
a few caraway seeds
2 cloves garlic, crushed
cold water - enough to prevent meat sticking

2 lb potatoes, cubed
2 large carrots, cubed
1 large green pepper, cubed
salt to taste

Method:

1   Melt dripping or oil in saucepan.
2   Fry onion for 5 minutes, add paprika and stir rapidly.
3   Add meat and salt, stirring constantly until browned.
4   Add caraway seeds, garlic and sufficient water.
5   Cover and braise slowly - **MUST NOT BE BOILED.**
6   Par-boil potatoes and carrots in a separate pan.
7   Drain, but reserve cooking liquid to top up stew pan.
8   Add potatoes, carrots and green pepper to meat and cook until tender, adding vegetable liquid as required.
9   Serve with crusty bread and green salad.

Zofie Victor, E.E.F.C., Hungary

Argyll Steaks

1 pkt tomato soup
1 pkt mushroom soup
1 Oxo cube
4 steaks (sirloin or fillet)

1 oz (25g) butter
2 onions, diced
8oz (225g) mushrooms, sliced

Method:

1   Mix powdered tomato and mushroom soups and rub in dry Oxo cube.
2   Coat steaks on both sides with the dry mixture and place in oven proof dish.
3   Melt butter in frying pan and fry onions until soft.
4   Remove onion with slotted spoon and place on top of steaks.
5   Fry mushrooms in the remaining butter until coated and place on steaks.
6   Cover and leave overnight in fridge, or for at least 2 hours.
7   Cook in pre-heated oven 160°C/325°F/Gas 3 for 1 hour or until tender.

Isbbel MacAuley, Assynt

Moussaka

1 large aubergine	2 tblsp tomato purée
salt and pepper	2 tblsp parsley, chopped
$^1/_4$ cup cooking oil	1 oz (25g) butter
2 onions, chopped	1 oz (25g) flour
2 cloves garlic, chopped	$^1/_2$ pt (300ml) milk
1 $^1/_4$ lb (550g) mince	1 egg, beaten
15 oz (425g) tin tomatoes	3 oz (75g) cheese, grated

Method:

1   Cut the aubergine into $^1/_2$" (5mm) slices and sprinkle with salt.
2   Place in colander for 30 minutes to drain excess moisture and then rinse and pat dry.
3   Heat half the oil and fry the aubergine slices until browned then set aside.
4   In remaining oil fry onion and garlic, add mince and brown.
5   Add tomatoes, purée, and parsley and simmer for 20 minutes.
6   Make white sauce with butter, flour and milk.
7   Season and stir in egg and half the cheese.
8   Layer aubergine and mince in a greased pie-dish, finishing with aubergine.
9   Pour over white sauce and sprinkle with remaining cheese.
10 Cook in a pre-heated oven 180°C/350°F/Gas 4 for 1$^1/_2$ hours.
    Serve with green salad and crusty bread.

Katie Graham, C.W.I., Australia

Beef Scone

8 oz (225g) corned beef	8 oz (225g) S. R. flour
2 level tblsp chutney	1 level tsp salt
4 level tblsp tomato sauce	2 oz (50g) margarine
	4-5 fl oz milk

Method:

1   Mash the corned beef, chutney and sauce thoroughly together.
2   Mix the flour and salt and rub in margarine.
3   Add milk to make a soft dough.
4   Knead lightly and roll into an oblong - 10" x 6" (250 x 150mm).
5   Brush round the edges (approx. $^1/_2$") with milk.
6   Spread the corned beef mixture over the dough, roll up as for a Swiss roll and seal the edges.
7   Place on a baking tray, pricking on top to allow steam to escape.
8   Bake in a pre-heated oven 220°C/425°F/Gas 7 for 20-30 minutes.

A. and C. Calder, Glensbiel

Basic Meat Loaf

8 oz (225g) mince	salt and pepper
6 oz (175g) smoked bacon, minced	Worcester sauce
3 oz (75g) white breadcrumbs	1 egg, beaten

Method:

1 Mix mince with bacon in large bowl.
2 Add breadcrumbs, seasoning and Worcester sauce.
3 Add egg to dry ingredients.
4 Press into bowl, cover and steam for 1–1¹/₂ hours.

B. K. Wemyss, Dingwall

Crunchy Meat Loaf

1 lb (450g) mince	1 tblsp Worcester sauce
6 oz (175g) white breadcrumbs	1 tblsp tomato juice
8 oz (225g) carrots, grated	1 tsp English mustard
1 small onion, chopped	1 tsp mixed herbs
1 clove garlic, crushed	1 egg (size 2), beaten
¹/₂ small pepper, finely chopped	salt and pepper to taste

Method:

1 Mix all ingredients together thoroughly.
2 Grease and line the base of a 6" ovenproof dish.
3 Spoon mixture into it, pressing it down firmly.,
4 Cook in a pre-heated oven 180°C/350°F/Gas 4 for 1¹/₂ hours.
5 Serve cold, cut in wedges like a cake.

Katie Moir, Partick Highland, Glasgow

Pork and Beef Loaf

8 oz (225g) mince	salt and pepper
8 oz (225g) sausage meat	1 egg, beaten
1 dsp white breadcrumbs	8 oz (225g) sliced, canned peaches
1 small onion, grated	2 tomatoes, cut in wedges
2 tblsp tomato ketchup	

Method:

1 Mix together mince, sausage meat, breadcrumbs, onion, ketchup, and seasoning and combine with egg.
2 Shape into a loaf and place in a baking dish.
3 Cook in a pre-heated oven 180°C/350°F/Gas 4 for 1–1¹/₂ hours.
4 Remove from dish and allow to cool.
5 Decorate with peach slices and tomato wedges.
6 Serve, sliced with hot buttered toast or crispy rolls.

Margaret MacKay, Bettyhill

Microwaved Minced Beef and Bean Casserole

1 onion, chopped
1 lb (450g) minced beef
9 oz (250g) baked beans
2 tblsp Worcester sauce

2 tblsp tomato purée
1/4 pt (150ml) beef stock
salt and pepper

Method:

1. Cook onion in covered dish for 3 minutes on "High".
2. Stir in mince, cover and cook for 5 minutes on "High".
3. Break up after 2 minutes and drain off excess fat.
4. Stir in beans, Worcester sauce, tomato purée, stock and seasoning.
5. Cover and cook on "High" for 15 minutes.

Anne Mackenzie, Tarbat, Portmahomack

Lemon Barbecued Meat Loaves (Microwaved)

8 oz (225g) mince
3 tblsp white breadcrumbs
1/2 small onion, chopped
1/2 tblsp lemon juice
salt and pepper
1/2 egg, beaten
2 thin slices lemon

Sauce:
2 oz (50g) soft dark brown sugar
pinch dry mustard
pinch all-spice
pinch ground cloves
2 tblsp tomato sauce

Method:

1. Combine mince, breadcrumbs, onions, lemon juice and seasoning and bind with beaten egg.
2. Press half the mixture into a cup and turn out on to a shallow baking dish. Repeat with remaining mixture.
3. Place 2 loaves, uncovered, in microwave and cook on "Full Power" for 3 minutes.
4. Remove from microwave, place a slice of lemon on each loaf.
5. Mix sauce ingredients and use to coat each loaf.
6. Again microwave, uncovered, at "Full Power" for 4 minutes. Allow 3 minutes standing time.

Chris MacKay, Govanhill, Glasgow

Irish Stew

6 lamb chops, trimmed	8 potatoes, sliced
1 tblsp oil	1 pt (600ml) stock
1 lb (450g) onions, sliced	salt and pepper
1 lb (450g) carrots, sliced	1 tblsp parsley, chopped
	chopped chives to garnish

Method:

1 Heat oil in frying pan; brown chops and remove from pan.
2 Sauté onions and carrots.
3 Put chops, onions and carrots into an ovenproof dish.
4 Cover with potatoes, add stock and seasoning.
5 Cover and cook in pre-heated oven 160°C/325°F/Gas 4 for 2 hours.
6 Garnish and serve immediately.

Mary Murray, North Tolsta, Lewis

Tomato Bredie

3 lb (1350g) breast of lamb, cut into bite-sized pieces
3 tsp flour
2 tsp cooking oil
2 onions, chopped
3 tsp salt and pinch black pepper
1 tsp sugar
2 lb (900g) ripe tomatoes, skinned and chopped
$^1/_2$ pt (300ml) stock

Method:

1 Roll the lamb in flour and brown in hot cooking oil.
2 Add onion and sauté until transparent.
3 Add all the remaining ingredients and simmer until the lamb is tender (2-2$^1/_2$ hours).
4 Add more liquid during cooking if required.
   (Note: A bredie is like a stew, but uses less water. It can be made using any other
       suitable vegetable in place of the tomatoes).

Ladies in King William's Town, South Africa

Crispy Leg of Lamb

3 ¹/₂ lbs (1575g) leg of lamb
2 garlic cloves, crushed
1 tsp cumin

¹/₄ pt (150ml) stock
4 oz (100g) breadcrumbs
salt and pepper

Method:

1 Heat oven to 230°C/450°F/Gas 8.
2 Rub lamb with garlic, cumin and seasoning.
3 Put into hot oven and roast for 20 minutes, then pour over stock.
4 Reduce heat to 180°C/350°F/Gas 4 and cook for approx. 1¹/₂ hours.
5 Turn off oven, remove lamb and cover joint with breadcrumbs.
6 Return to oven and brown for a further 15 minutes.
7 Serve with roast potatoes, broccoli and glazed onions.

J. Nicolson, Lochs, Lewis

Lamb Rolls Billabong

12 lamb chops, boned
6 rashers bacon

1 tblsp flour
1 egg
4 oz (100g) breadcrumbs
oil as required
12 pineapple rings

Method:

1 Wrap half rashers of bacon round each chop.
2 Dip each chop into flour, egg and breadcrumbs in turn.
3 Place on baking tray and brush with oil.
4 Bake in pre-heated oven 180°C/350°F/Gas 4 for 30 minutes.
5 Serve on pineapple rings with supreme sauce.

Supreme Sauce:

1 tblsp butter
4 oz (100g) mushrooms, sliced
1 chicken stock cube

¹/₂ cup shallots, chopped
¹/₂ cup tomato soup
¹/₂ cup double cream

Method:

1 Melt butter, fry mushrooms and add crumbled stock cube.
2 Add shallots and soup and simmer for 20 minutes.
3 Add cream and serve with chops.

Grace Harris, St George's, Sydney, Australia

Sweet and Sour Lamb Chops

4 lamb chops

1 dsp oil

2 oz (50g) mushrooms

1/2 red pepper, sliced

1/2 green pepper, sliced

2 carrots, cut in sticks

1 small can pineapple

1 tblsp vinegar

2 tblsp soy sauce

1 tsp black pepper

1 dsp brown sugar

2 tsp cornflour

Method:

1 Heat oil in large frying pan and fry chops quickly.
2 Add rest of ingredients (except cornflour) to pan and bring to boil.
3 Simmer for 30 minutes.
4 Blend cornflour in a little water, add to pan and stir until thickened.
5 Serve with rice (or potatoes) and salad.

D. Shaw, Callanish, Lewis

A Cheap Roast

Breast of lamb, boned

Stuffing:

1 oz (25g) dripping

1 onion, chopped

3 oz (75g) breadcrumbs

1 oz (25g) suet (or oil)

1 tsp parsley

1 tsp mint

1 tsp fresh rosemary (optional)

1 tsp salt and pepper

1 egg, beaten

Method:

1 Melt dripping and lightly fry onion until soft.
2 Mix in dry ingredients and sufficient egg to obtain a stiff consistency.
3 Spread stuffing on lamb and roll up like a Swiss roll.
4 Secure with fine string.
5 Place in roasting tin and cook in pre-heated oven 180°C/350°F/Gas 4 for 35 minutes per lb (stuffed weight)

I. Smith, Grant St., Glasgow

Sweet and Sour Pork Chops

4 spare rib pork chops
8 oz (225g) long grained rice, cooked

Sauce:

1 oz (25g) margarine
1 small onion, chopped
1 small green pepper,
    deseeded and chopped
7 oz (200g) tin pineapple, chopped

2 tsp Worcester sauce
2 tblsp demerara sugar
2 tblsp tomato ketchup
1 tblsp sweet chutney
2 tblsp malt vinegar
1 tblsp cornflour
$^1/_2$ tsp salt

Method:

1   Melt margarine in a saucepan and fry onion and pepper for 3 minutes.
2   Strain pineapple juice and make up to $^1/_2$ pint with water.
3   Add pineapple and juice to pan.
4   Stir in Worcester sauce, sugar, ketchup and chutney.
5   Blend together vinegar and cornflour and add to pan with salt.
6   Bring to boil, stirring and cook for 1 minute.
7   Pour sauce into a 2 pint casserole and arrange chops on top.
8   Cover and cook in a pre-heated oven 200°C/400°F/Gas 6 for 1 hour, removing lid for
    last 15 minutes.
9   Serve chops on warm serving dish, surrounded with rice and covered with sauce. Put
    remaining sauce in sauce boat.

Grace Fraser, Cumbernauld

Savoury Pork Chops

4 pork chops
1 oz (25g) cooking oil
12 oz (350g) onions, sliced
4 tomatoes, sliced
8 oz (225g) cooking apples, peeled and sliced

pinch mixed herbs
$^1/_4$ pt (150ml) stock
salt and pepper

Method:

1   Wipe chops and quickly fry in oil until brown on both sides.
2   Place onions, tomatoes and apples in an ovenproof dish and sprinkle with mixed herbs.
3   Place chops on top, add stock, and sprinkle with seasoning.
4   Cover and cook in a pre-heated oven 180°C/350°F/Gas 4 for 1$^1/_2$ hours.

Morag Graham, Partick Highland, Glasgow

Pork Parcels

4 x 6 oz (175g) pork steaks
6 oz (175g) courgettes, thinly sliced
1 cooking apple, peeled and chopped
7 oz (200g) tin tomatoes
1 tblsp tomato purée
1 tsp ground sage
salt and pepper

Method:

1   Mix all ingredients (except steaks) in a bowl.
2   Place steaks in foil, cover with the mixture and parcel up.
3   Cook in a pre-heated oven 180°C/350°F/Gas 4 for 1 hour.

Chris Ina MacLeod, Lochs, Lewis

Pork with Spiced Apricots

$^1/_2$ pt (300ml) orange juice
4 oz (100g) dried apricots
4 pork fillets or loin chops
2 tblsp olive oil
1 rounded tblsp cornflour
$^1/_4$ tsp cinnamon

$^1/_4$ pt (150ml) white wine
salt and pepper
7 oz (200g) carton soft cream cheese
1 tblsp chopped parsley or chives

Method:

1   Soak apricots overnight in orange juice.
2   Brown pork in oil and place in casserole dish.
3   Blend cornflour and cinnamon in remaining oil while gradually adding apricots and juice.
4   Bring to boil, cook until thickened, gradually adding wine and seasoning.
5   Pour sauce over meat and cook in a pre-heated oven 160°C/325°F/Gas 3 for 45-60 minutes.
6   Mix cream cheese and parsley together until soft and stir into casserole just before serving.

Marietta MacDonald, Carloway, Lewis

Pork Chops with Scalloped Potatoes

4 pork chops
1 tblsp cooking oil
salt and pepper

1 tin cream of mushroom soup
$^1/_2$ cup sour cream
$^1/_2$ cup water
4 cups potatoes, thinly sliced

Method:

1 Combine soup, sour cream and water.
2 Alternate layers of potatoes and soup mixture in greased 4 pint casserole and cover with lid.
3 Bake in a pre-heated oven 190°C/375°F/Gas 5 for 45 minutes.
4 Sprinkle chops with seasoning, brown in oil and place on top of potato mixture.
5 Return casserole to oven and cook for a further 30 minutes.

Judy Honeycutt, Buccleuch & Greyfriars, Edinburgh

Pork Chops In Cider

1 large onion, sliced
3 apples, peeled and sliced
4 pork chops or fillets
salt and pepper
$^1/_4$ pt (150ml) cider or apple juice

3 oz (75g) breadcrumbs
3 oz (75g) cheese, grated

Method:

1 Place onion and apple in layers in ovenproof dish.
2 Arrange chops on top, season and pour over cider.
3 Mix together breadcrumbs and cheese and spread over dish.
4 Cover and bake in a pre-heated oven 180°C/350°F/Gas 4 for 1 $^1/_2$ hours, removing cover for last 30 minutes to brown.

Mairi MacKay, Stornoway, Lewis

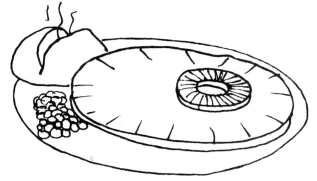

Cumberland Steaks

4 ham steaks
1/2 oz (12g) butter
salt and pepper
1 lemon
1 orange

2 tsp cornflour
4-5 tblsp redcurrant jelly
pinch dry mustard
pinch ground ginger

Method:

1 Place knob of butter on each steak, season and grill for 5 minutes on each side.
2 Pare several lengths of rind from orange and lemon, cut into fine strips and blanch for 5 minutes.
3 Mix cornflour in a little water and put into saucepan with juice of orange and lemon, redcurrant jelly, mustard and ginger.
4 Heat slowly, stirring until jelly melts and sauce thickens.
5 Drain rinds and add to hot sauce.
6 Place in jug and serve at once with the steaks.

Janet Morrison, Stoer

Carrot and Bacon Roulade

4 eggs, separated
1 tblsp plain flour
1 tblsp whole grain mustard
8 oz (225g) carrots, cooked

8 oz (225g) back bacon
7 oz (200g) cream cheese
1 tblsp mayonnaise

Method:

1 Place the egg yolks, flour, mustard and carrots in a processor and blend until smooth.
2 Whisk egg whites and fold into carrot mixture.
3 Pour into a greased 7" x 11" tin and bake in a pre-heated oven 200°C/400°F/Gas 6 for 12-15 minutes.
4 Remove from tin on to a sheet of greaseproof paper, roll up like a Swiss roll and allow to cool.
5 Grill bacon, cut into pieces and mix with cream cheese and mayonnaise.
6 Unroll the roulade, spread on filling and re-roll carefully.
7 Chill for 1 hour before serving.

Ina MacLeod, Kyle

Supper Sausage Roll

1 lb (450g) pork sausagemeat
8 oz (225g) boiled potatoes, mashed
1 small onion, chopped
2 celery stalks, chopped
1 tsp curry powder
1 tsp tomato ketchup
salt and pepper

13 oz (375g) packet of puff pastry
milk to glaze

Method:

1 Place sausagemeat, potatoes, onion, celery, curry powder, ketchup and seasoning in a large bowl.
2 Combine and form into a 10" roll.
3 Roll out pastry into a rectangle, 8" x 10".
4 Place meat roll on to pastry, damp edges and roll up.
5 Cut into required sizes.
6 Place on baking tray, brush with milk and score with knife.
7 Bake in a pre-heated oven 200°C/400°F/Gas 6 for 45 minutes.
8 Serve with salad.

Joan Smith, Cross, Lewis

Farm House Flan

Pastry:

3 oz (75g) plain wholemeal flour
3 oz (75g) S. R. flour
pinch of salt
1 1/2 oz (40g) butter
1 1/2 oz (40g) lard
3 tblsp milk

Filling:

3 oz (75g) leeks, chopped
4 oz (100g) bacon, chopped
1/2 oz (12g) butter
3 oz (75g) cheddar cheese, grated
2 eggs
1/4 pt (150ml) milk
salt and pepper

Method:

1 To make pastry, rub butter and lard into flour and salt to resemble breadcrumbs. Bind together with milk, knead lightly and chill for 20 minutes.
2 Roll out pastry, use to line an 8" flan dish and bake blind in a pre-heated oven 200°C/400°F/Gas 6-7 for 10-15 minutes.
3 Sauté leeks and bacon in butter until soft.
4 Place on base of flan and sprinkle with most of the cheese.
5 Beat together eggs, milk and seasoning and pour on to flan.
6 Cover with rest of cheese, return to oven and bake until set.
7 Serve hot or cold with salad.

Alice Ross, Lybster

Quick Wholemeal Pizza

Base:
8 oz (225g) S. R. wholemeal flour
2 oz (50g) butter/margarine
pinch of salt
milk to mix

Topping:
1 large onion, chopped
14 oz (400g) tin tomatoes,
   sieved and chopped
1 tin sweetcorn
ham/bacon, chopped
green/red pepper, chopped
cheddar cheese, grated

Method:

1   To make base, rub butter into flour and salt.
    Bind together with sufficient milk and roll out on to a greased pizza plate.
2   Sauté onion and scatter over pizza dough.
3   Add all topping ingredients and cover thickly with cheese.
4   Bake in a pre-heated oven 200°C/400°F/Gas 6 for $^1/_2$ hour or more.

Maureen Murray, Rogart

Quickie Pizza

Base:
6 oz (175g) S. R. flour
$^1/_2$ tsp salt
1 $^1/_2$ oz (40g) butter
$^1/_4$ tsp mixed herbs
6 tblsp milk

Topping:
1 oz (25g) butter
1 large onion, sliced
4 rashers streaky bacon,
   cut into pieces
2 tomatoes, chopped
6 oz (175g) cheese, grated

Method:

1   To make base, rub butter into sifted flour and salt.
    Add herbs and mix to a soft dough with milk.
    Knead, roll out into a large circle and place on a greased baking tray.
2   Sauté onion in 1 oz butter until soft, place on pizza base.
3   Pile on all other ingredients and top with grated cheese.
4   Bake in a pre-heated oven 220°C/425°F/Gas 7 for 30 minutes.

Christy MacKinnon, Scalpay, Harris

 *Chicken*

Oven Baked Chicken

4 chicken portions, skinned
2 oz (50g) butter
2 1/2 oz (60g) pkt. plain crisps
4 oz (100g) grated cheese

1 tblsp parsley
1/4 tsp garlic powder
1/2 tsp dried tarragon
salt and pepper

Method:

1   Melt butter and brush half of it over chicken.
2   Crush crisps and mix with remaining ingredients, seasoning to taste.
3   Press this mixture around chicken portions and place them on a baking tray or in an ovenproof dish.
4   Sprinkle over the remaining butter.
5   Bake in pre-heated oven 180°C/350°F/Gas 4 for 45 minutes. (Or until chicken is tender and juices run clear).
6   Serve with a baked potato and sweetcorn or a side salad with crusty bread.

A. Hughson, Stornoway, Lewis

Caribbean Chicken

1 tblsp oil
2 chicken joints, skinned
2 oz (50g) cashew nuts
2 oz (50g) onions, chopped
2 oz (50g) mushrooms, chopped
3 oz (75g) green pepper, sliced
salt and pepper

2 tsp cornflour
2 tblsp pineapple juice
10 fl oz chicken stock
2 rings canned pineapple
2 tsp curry powder
2 tsp tomato ketchup
1 medium banana, sliced

Method:

1   Heat oil in pan and brown chicken joints.
2   Remove chicken and place in casserole with nuts.
3   Brown onions, mushrooms and peppers in pan, add to chicken and season.
4   Blend cornflour with pineapple juice.
5   Pour, with stock, into pan and add all other remaining ingredients (except banana).
6   Bring to boil and pour sauce over chicken and vegetables.
7   Bake in pre-heated oven 180°C/350°F/Gas 4 for 1 hour.
8   Add banana and serve with rice.

M. MacAskill, Dunblane

Barbecue Chicken

8 chicken drumsticks
or 4 chicken portions
1 tsp salt

2 tblsp soy sauce
2 tblsp vegetable oil
3 drops Tabasco sauce
2 cloves garlic, crushed

Sauce:

1" fresh root ginger,
  peeled and chopped
$^1/_2$ pt (300ml) tomato juice

2 tsp cornflour
3 tblsp red wine vinegar
1 tsp brown sugar

Method:

1 Season chicken with salt.
2 Mix together soy sauce, oil, Tabasco and garlic and coat the chicken.
3 Place in shallow ovenproof dish.
4 Bake in pre-heated oven 200°C/400°F/Gas 6 for approx. 50 minutes, basting occasionally.

Sauce:

1 Cook ginger in oil for 2 minutes.
2 Blend a little of the tomato juice with cornflour, then stir in the remainder of juice.
3 Add to pan and bring to boil, stirring until thickening.
4 Stir in red wine vinegar and brown sugar.
5 Pour sauce over chicken and serve.

Donald Nicolson, Greenock

Honey Chicken

8 chicken thighs, skinned
8 tblsp corn oil
2 onions, sliced
1 large carrot, peeled and thinly sliced
1 green pepper, chopped

2 tblsp flour
$^3/_4$ pt (425ml) chicken stock
1 tblsp clear honey
1 tblsp soy sauce

Method:

1 Heat oil in large, flameproof casserole dish.
2 Brown chicken and remove from dish.
3 Brown onions, add carrot and pepper and cook until soft.
4 Stir in flour and cook for 1 minute.
5 Add stock gradually, stir in honey and soy sauce.
6 Bring to boil, add chicken pieces.
7 Cover and cook in pre-heated oven 190°C/375°F/Gas 5 for 60-75 minutes.

Marina MacLeod, Struan, Skye

Chicken Simla

4 chicken breasts, scored

Marinade:

1 tsp curry powder
2 tblsp soft brown sugar
$^1/4$ tsp salt
1 tblsp lemon juice

Sauce:

2 tblsp mango or apple, chutney
2 fl oz water
dash of Worcester sauce

Method:

1   Mix marinade ingredients and pour over chicken.
2   Leave for 2 hours at least, preferably overnight.
3   Grill at moderate heat, or oven cook chicken at 180°C/350°F/Gas 4.
4   Put sauce ingredients in pan, bring to boil.
5   Serve with the chicken on a bed of rice.

Vina Campbell, Free North, Inverness

Thai Chicken

8 chicken breasts or quarters
1lb (450g) onions, chopped
2 large garlic cloves, chopped
2 x 14 oz (400g) tins tomatoes
4 oz (100g) crunchy peanut butter
$^1/2$ oz (12g) flour

1 tsp brown sugar
1 tsp ground cardamum
1 $^1/2$ tsp turmeric
2 tsp cumin
$^1/4$-$^1/2$ tsp chilli powder
4 tblsp vinegar
5 tblsp soya sauce

Method:

1   Arrange chicken in casserole dish.
2   Fry onions and garlic, blend in tomatoes and peanut butter.
3   Add rest of ingredients to pan and mix together.
4   Pour over chicken and cover.
5   Bake in pre-heated oven 180°C/350°F/Gas 4 for 2 hours, stirring occasionally.
6   Serve with rice.

Mairi MacLeod, Bon Accord, Aberdeen

Chicken and Plum Casserole

4 chicken joints, browned
1 onion, chopped
1 tblsp oil
salt and pepper

$^1/2$ pt (300ml) chicken stock
2 tsp ground ginger
1 tin plums

Method:

1   Fry onion in oil and add to browned chicken in casserole.
2   Add salt and pepper and stock.
3   Sprinkle with ginger, add strained plums around chicken joints.
4   Bake in pre-heated oven 180°C/350°F/Gas 4 for 1 hour.

Cathie Martin, Grant St., Glasgow

Uncle George's Satay Chicken

8 chicken fillets
1 onion, chopped
1 garlic clove, chopped
1 tblsp oil
$^1/_2$ cup chicken stock

$^1/_4$ cup peanut butter
$^1/_4$ cup honey
2 tsp grainy mustard
1 tsp curry powder
dash of Tabasco

Method:

1 Cook onion and garlic in a little oil for a few minutes.
2 Remove from pan and set aside.
3 Brown chicken in pan, add stock, onion and garlic mixture.
4 Add rest of ingredients and cook slowly until dish is thick and saucy with a good aroma.

Lady MacAulay, Elder Memorial, Leith

Broccoli Chicken

1 lb (450g) cooked chicken, chopped
7 oz (200g) cooked broccoli florets
15 oz (440g) tin Campbell's cream of chicken soup
2 tsp curry powder
2 tsp lemon juice
4 tblsp mayonnaise
1 cup mature cheddar cheese, grated
$^3/_4$ cup breadcrumbs

Method:

1 Grease large ovenproof dish, spread chicken on base and cover with broccoli.
2 Combine soup, curry powder, lemon juice and mayonnaise in bowl and pour over chicken and broccoli.
3 Combine cheese and breadcrumbs and sprinkle over mixture.
4 Bake, uncovered, in pre-heated oven 160°C/350°F/Gas 3 for 45 minutes.
5 Serve with appropriate vegetables and roast potatoes. *Maxwell House, Eventide Home, Glasgow*

Mango Chicken

cooked chicken (from approx. 3 lb bird)
$^1/_2$ pt (300ml) mayonnaise
$^1/_4$ pt (150ml) natural Greek yoghurt or cream
1 tsp curry powder
$^1/_2$ jar Mango Chutney - chop the large pieces

Method:

1 Cut chicken into bite-sized pieces.
2 Combine mayonnaise, yoghurt, curry powder and Mango Chutney
3 Heat gently until blended, then fold in chicken pieces.
4 Serve hot or cold with rice. *Marilyn MacDonald, St. Vincent St. - Milton, Glasgow*

Chicken Tarragon

4 chicken breasts,
  boned and skinned
1 tblsp cooking oil
1 cup white wine
  (or chicken stock)

1 tblsp tomato purée
1 tblsp soy sauce
3-4 sprigs tarragon (or 2 tsp dried)
4 fl oz single cream
pinch salt and black pepper

Method:

1 Fry chicken gently in oil in a flat or large pan, but do not brown.
2 Add wine, purée and soy sauce.
3 Add half the tarragon and season to taste.
4 Simmer gently for 30-40 minutes in a covered pan.
5 Immediately before serving, turn off heat and stir in remaining tarragon and cream.
6 Serve with jacket or salad potatoes, green beans or mange tout.

Isobel McQueer, Tain

Roast Pheasant With Oatmeal Stuffing

1 brace young pheasants
2 oz (50g) medium oatmeal
1 small onion, finely chopped
2 oz (50g) sharp eating apple,
  peeled and chopped
1 oz (25g) shredded suet
1 egg yolk
salt and pepper

1 oz (25g) butter, melted
6 oz (175g) streaky bacon
2 tblsp plain flour
1/2 pt (300ml) game stock
2 fl oz red wine
1 tblsp soy sauce

Method:

1 Wipe pheasants inside and outside and season cavity.
2 Toast oatmeal until golden brown.
3 Mix with onion, apple, suet and egg yolk and season well.
4 Spoon mixture inside birds and tie up.
5 Place birds in roasting tin and brush well with butter.
6 Wrap bacon over birds.
7 Roast in pre-heated oven 220°C/425°F/Gas 7 for 45 minutes, basting frequently.
8 Remove bacon and roast for a further 10 minutes.
9 Add flour to juices in roasting tin to thicken, then add stock and wine to make gravy.

C. MacLeod, Lochs, Lewis

Pasta

Tallarines Verdes (Green Spaghetti)

12 oz (350g) spaghetti
salted water
little oil
8 oz (225g) spinach
$^1/_2$ large tin evaporated milk
$^1/_2$ tsp garlic powder

8 oz (225g) cottage cheese
$^1/_2$ tsp chilli powder
1 tblsp onion, chopped
1 tblsp salted peanuts
$^1/_2$ tsp basil
salt and pepper

Method:

1 Boil spaghetti in plenty salted water and a little oil.
2 Remove stalks from spinach, boil in very little water for 1 minute and strain well.
3 Place milk in food processor, add garlic, cheese and chilli powder and blend.
4 Add spinach, then onion, nuts and basil and season to taste.
5 Strain spaghetti well when cooked.
6 Combine sauce and spaghetti in a large pan, heat and serve.

Gillian Silva, London

Spaghetti Alla Carbonara

5 eggs
4 fl oz (120ml) double cream
salt and pepper
1 tblsp olive oil
1 oz (25g) butter

7 oz (200g) streaky bacon, diced
1 lb (450g) spaghetti
4 oz (100g) cheese, grated
freshly ground pepper

Method:

1 Beat eggs and cream together with seasoning.
2 Heat oil and butter and gently fry bacon.
3 Cook spaghetti, drain, add to bacon and stir well.
4 Remove from heat and stir in eggs and cream with a small quantity of the cheese.
5 Stir gently until each strand is coated with the thick yellow cream.
6 Stir in remaining cheese and ground pepper.
7 Serve at once.

Catriona Ferguson, Tarbat, Portmahomack

 *Pasta*

Pasta Twists in Chicken and Cream Sauce

6 oz (175g) pasta twists
1 tblsp oil
12 oz (350g) chicken breasts, cut in strips
1 onion, chopped
2 cloves garlic, crushed
4 oz (100g) mushrooms, quartered
$^1/_2$ red pepper, deseeded and chopped
$^1/_4$ pt (150ml) dry white wine
$^1/_2$ pt (300ml) single cream
salt and pepper

Method:

1　Cook pasta according to instructions.
2　Heat oil and fry chicken for 5 minutes.
3　Add onion, garlic, mushroom and pepper and lightly fry for 5 minutes.
4　Add wine and simmer for further 10 minutes.
5　Add cream and seasoning and simmer for further 10 minutes.
6　Add drained pasta twists and serve.

Morag Macleod, Helmsdale

Saucy Pasta Spirals

4 rashers streaky bacon, chopped
1 tblsp oil
1 large onion, finely chopped
1 clove garlic, crushed
1 small green or red pepper, finely chopped
1 lb (450g) lean minced beef
1 large carrot, finely sliced
1 tsp dried thyme
1 tblsp tomato purée
4 tblsp red wine or beef stock
12 oz (350g) pasta spirals or shells
salt and pepper
1 spring onion for garnish, finely chopped

Method:

1　Fry bacon in its own fat in a heavy based pan until lightly coloured.
2　Add oil (if necessary), onion, garlic and pepper and cook until soft.
3　Add mince and cook until browned.
4　Add carrot, thyme, purée and wine or stock and cook for 25 minutes.
5　Meanwhile cook pasta in a large pan of salted boiling water and drain.
6　Season the sauce and serve over the pasta.
7　Garnish with spring onion.

I. Sutherland, Lairg

Marzette

1 lb (450g) steak mince
2 onions, chopped
1 tin condensed cream of tomato soup
1 tin condensed cream of mushroom soup
seasoning or crushed stock cube
5 oz (150g) cheese, grated
4 oz (100g) egg noodles (boiled in salted water)

Method:

1   Brown mince in pan, add onions, soups, seasoning and cheese.
2   Add cooked noodles and transfer to a casserole dish.
3   Bake in a pre-heated oven at 180°C/350°F/Gas 4 for 1 hour.
    (Note: This can be prepared early, stored in the fridge and cooked later for 1 hour.)

Elizabeth Macleod, Elder Memorial, Leith

Quick Beef with Macaroni

1 tblsp oil
2 onions, sliced
1 clove garlic, crushed
1 lb (450g) minced beef
1 tsp dried oregano
6 oz (175g) quick cooking macaroni,
    cooked and drained

14 oz (400g) tin tomatoes
2 tblsp tomato purée
salt
2 tsp paprika
3 oz (75g) cheddar cheese, sliced

Method:

1   Fry onions and garlic in oil until soft.
2   Stir in beef and fry until browned.
3   Add oregano, macaroni, tomatoes, purée, salt and paprika and bring to the boil.
4   Place in a casserole dish and arrange cheese slices on top.
5   Bake in a pre-heated oven at 180°C/350°F/Gas 4 for 20 minutes or until browned.

Mary Murray, Partick Highland, Glasgow

 *Pasta*

Lasagne

Meat sauce:	**White sauce:**
1 lb (450g) mince	2 oz (50g) butter
1 onion, chopped	2 oz (50g) plain flour
14 oz (400g) can chopped tomatoes	1pt (600ml) milk
1 tblsp tomato purée	
1 clove garlic	lasagne
1 tsp basil	parmesan cheese
salt and pepper	

Method:

1 Combine all ingredients for meat sauce and simmer for 30 minutes.
2 Melt butter, add flour, add milk slowly, cook until thick and smooth.
3 In a square dish, arrange layers of meat sauce, lasagne and white sauce finishing with white sauce.
4 Sprinkle cheese generously on top and cook in a pre-heated oven at 180°C/350°F/Gas 4 for 30 minutes.

E Murchison, Ardelve

Tuna and Mushroom Lasagne

8 oz (225g) mushrooms, sliced	salt and pepper
3 oz (75g) butter	juice $^1/_2$ lemon
2 oz (50g) plain flour	lasagne
1 $^1/_2$ pts (900ml) milk	3 oz (75g) cheese, grated
2 x 8 oz (225g) tins tuna, drained	

Method:

1 Sauté mushrooms in butter, add flour, stir over heat for 1 minute.
2 Add milk gradually, removing from heat when sauce bubbles.
3 Stir in tuna, seasoning and juice.
4 Spoon some sauce into greased ovenproof dish, then place on top a sheet of lasagne which has been dipped in hot water.
5 Continue to layer sauce and lasagne, ending with sauce.
6 Sprinkle with cheese and bake in a pre-heated oven at 180°C/350°F/Gas 4 for 20-25 minutes.

Fiona MacKeddie, Maryburgh

Tuna and Pasta Bake

1 1/2 oz (40g) butter or margarine
1 1/2 oz (40g) plain flour
1 pt (600ml) milk
pinch of salt
4 tblsp tomato sauce
2 large tins tuna, drained
1 medium tin sweetcorn
1 cup pasta, cooked
tomato or prawn cocktail flavoured crisps, crushed

Method:

1 Melt butter, stir in flour, then add milk gradually until sauce is thick and smooth, seasoning to taste.
2 Add all other ingredients (except crisps) and mix well.
3 Place in an ovenproof dish and bake in a pre-heated oven at 180°C/350°F/Gas 4 for 20-30 minutes.
4 Sprinkle with crisps prior to serving with baked potatoes.

Joan Macleod, Partick Highland, Glasgow

Mushroom Rice Toss

2 tblsp butter
1 onion, chopped
4 rashers bacon, chopped
1 red pepper, chopped
1 clove garlic, crushed

9 oz (250g) mushrooms, sliced
4 cups cooked rice
salt and pepper
1/2 cup grated cheese
2 tblsp chopped parsley

Method:

1 Fry onions, bacon and pepper in butter in large pan until soft.
2 Add garlic and mushrooms and fry until mushrooms are tender.
3 Add rice and toss over a moderate heat.
4 Add cheese and seasoning, toss and top with parsley.

Letitia Ducasse, St George's P.C.E.A., Sydney, Australia

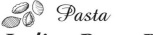 *Pasta*

Italian Pasta Bake

8 oz (225g) penne pasta (quills)
10 oz (275g) ham, cut into strips
3 eggs, beaten
³/4 pt (425ml) single cream

salt and pepper
5 oz (150g) Gruyere cheese, grated
2 oz (50g) parmesan cheese, grated

Method:

1 Boil pasta in salted water until just tender (approx 9 minutes), then drain.
2 Add ham and transfer to greased baking dish.
3 Beat together eggs and cream, add half the Gruyére cheese, season and pour over pasta.
4 Top with remaining cheeses and bake in a pre-heated oven at 190°C/375°F/Gas 5 until golden (approx 40 minutes).

Donald Nicolson, Greenock

Macaroni Mixture

There are no set amounts for this recipe

macaroni
onions, chopped
tomatoes, chopped

bacon, chopped
cheese, grated

Method:

1 Boil the usual amount of macaroni that you use for your household and drain.
2 Fry onions, tomatoes and bacon, mix into the macaroni and place in a flat dish.
3 Sprinkle with cheese and bake in pre-heated oven at 200°C/400°F/Gas 6 for 30 minutes.

John McIvor, Urray

Desserts

Banana Custard Flan

Pastry:

8 oz (225g) plain flour
5 oz (150g) margarine
1 egg, beaten
1 oz (25g) caster sugar

Meringue:

3 egg whites
6 oz (175g) caster sugar

Custard:

1 oz (25g) margarine
1 oz (25g) flour
1 pt (600ml) milk
2 oz (50g) brown sugar
3 egg yolks
2 bananas, sliced

Method:

1 Rub margarine into flour, add egg and sugar and knead gently.
2 Roll out pastry and use to line a flan tin.
3 Bake blind in a pre-heated oven 180°C/350°F/Gas 4 until cooked, but not coloured.
4 Melt margarine in pan, stir in flour, add milk and stir until thickened.
5 Add brown sugar, egg yolks and bananas and mix together.
6 Pour mixture into flan case and return to oven for a further 15 minutes.
7 Beat egg whites until stiff, add sugar and spread meringue over custard.
8 Return to oven and cook until golden brown.   *Janet Reid, Lochs, Lewis*

Apple Crumble Shorties

3 oz (75g) butter
3 oz (75g) caster sugar
8 oz (225g) plain flour
1 tsp baking powder
3 oz (75g) ground almonds
1 egg, beaten

Filling:

3 apples, peeled and chopped
14 oz (400g) tin Cherry Pie Filling
icing sugar to dust

Method:

1 Cream butter and sugar until light and fluffy.
2 Add flour, baking powder and ground almonds.
3 Beat in egg until large crumbs form.
4 Spoon half the mixture into a lightly greased, loose-based tin and press down.
5 Mix apples with pie filling and spread over base.
6 Using fingertips rub the remaining crumbs until finer and sprinkle over filling.
7 Bake in a pre-heated oven 180°C/350°F/Gas 4 for 40-45 minutes or until golden brown.
8 Dust with icing sugar and serve hot or cold with cream.   *Winnie Sutherland, Strathy*

Apricot Caramel Crumble

15 oz (425g) tin apricots
1 oz (25g) butter
2 oz (50g) brown sugar
1 oz (25g) flour
$^1/_2$ pt (300ml) milk
1 egg, separated

Crumble:

2 oz (50g) butter
2 oz (50g) S.R. flour
pinch of salt
2 oz (50g) cake crumbs
1 oz (25g) brown sugar
2 oz (25g) coconut

Method:

1   Drain apricots and place in a 3 pint ovenproof dish.
2   Melt butter and sugar and stir in flour and milk.
3   Boil slightly, stirring all the time.
4   Cool slightly and stir in egg yolk.
5   Beat egg white until stiff and fold into mixture.
6   Pour sauce over apricots.
7   To make crumble, rub butter into sifted flour and salt, mix in remaining ingredients and sprinkle over apricots.
8   Bake in a pre-heated oven 180°C/350°F/Gas 4 for 35-40 minutes.   *Dolina MacKinnon, Kilmorack*

Orange and Rhubarb Crumble

1 lb (450g) rhubarb, cut in 1" slices
grated juice and rind of 1 orange

Crumble:

3 oz (75g) margarine
5 oz (150g) plain flour
3 oz (75g) brown sugar

$^1/_2$ tsp ground ginger
1 oz (25g) rolled oats

Method:

1   Place rhubarb, rind and juice of orange in an ovenproof dish.
2   Rub margarine into flour and add sugar, ginger and oats.
3   Sprinkle crumble over rhubarb.
4   Bake in a pre-heated oven 190°C/375°F/Gas 5 for 40 minutes.   *Mary MacRae, Lochs, Lewis*

Baked Apple and Almond Pudding

1 lb (450g) cooking apples, sliced
2 oz (50g) soft brown sugar

4 oz (100g) butter
4 oz (100g) caster sugar
2 eggs, beaten
4 oz (100g) ground almonds

Method:

1   Arrange sliced apples and brown sugar in an ovenproof dish.
2   Cream butter and sugar, add eggs and fold in ground almonds.
3   Spread mixture evenly on top of apples.
4   Bake in a pre-heated oven 180°C/350°F/Gas 4 for 1 hour.   *J. Johnstone, Paisley*

Special Bread and Butter Pudding

4 slices bread, buttered
4 oz (100g) mixed dried fruit
2 oz (50g) caster sugar
15 oz (425) tin custard
$^1/4$ tsp grated nutmeg

Method:

1   Grease a 2 pint ovenproof dish.
2   Cut bread into triangles and arrange in alternative layers with fruit and half the sugar.
3   Pour custard over the dish and leave to stand for 30 minutes.
4   Mix nutmeg with remaining sugar and sprinkle on top.
5   Cook in a pre-heated oven 160°C/325°F/Gas 3 for 30 minutes.
6   Serve hot with cream.

Margaret Noble, Ferintosh

Steamed Syrup Pudding

2 tblsp syrup
6 oz (175g) S. R. flour
2 oz (50g) sugar
3 oz (75g) margarine

1 egg, beaten
$^1/2$ tsp lemon juice
$^1/4$ pt (150ml) milk

Method:

1   Put syrup in bottom of greased pudding bowl.
2   Mix dry ingredients in a bowl and rub in margarine.
3   Add egg, lemon juice and milk and mix to a soft consistency.
4   Put mixture over syrup and cover bowl with greaseproof paper.
5   Steam in pan of boiling water for $1^1/2$ hours.
    (Note: Do not allow water to dry out.)

Ella Ross, Bon Accord, Aberdeen

Christmas Pudding

1 cup plain flour
$^1/2$ level tsp bicarbonate of soda
1 cup margarine, chilled and grated
1 cup white breadcrumbs
2 eggs, beaten

1 cup currants
1 cup sultanas
1 cup raisins
1 cup carrot, grated
1 cup potato, grated
1 cup demerara sugar

Method:

1   Mix all ingredients together, put into a 2 $^1/2$ pint pudding basin and cover with greaseproof paper.
2   Place in pan of boiling water and steam for 1 hour if using pressure cooker (at 15 lb) or 3 hours in ordinary pan.

J. Johnstone, Paisley

65

Clootie Dumpling

To make a clootie dumpling you will need:
a large pan of boiling water
a side plate to put beneath the dumpling in the pan
a square of cloth, approx. 24" x 30"
and a length of string

Basic Recipe

1 lb (450g) plain flour
8 oz (225g) suet
8 oz (225g) sugar
8 oz (225g) raisins
8 oz (225g) currants

2 level tsp ginger
2 level tsp cinnamon
2 level tsp mixed spice
2 level dsp marmalade
2 level dsp syrup
2 level tsp bicarbonate of soda,
mixed with a little milk

Method:

1   Mix all the above ingredients together, lastly adding the bicarbonate of soda and milk.
2   Add more milk and mix well to make a fairly slack dough.
3   See opposite page for cooking instructions.

Richer Recipe

To make a richer dumpling add the following ingredients to the above recipe and
mix well:

8 oz (225g) mixed dried fruit
2 cooking apples, grated
2 carrots, grated
juice and zest of 1 orange

4 oz (100g) breadcrumbs
6 oz (175g) melted treacle
2 eggs, beaten

Mary MacMillan, Buccleuch & Greyfriars, Edinburgh

Family Clootie Dumpling

1 ¹/₂ lb (675g) S. R. flour	6 oz (175g) suet
12 oz (350g) mixed fruit	12 oz (35og) sugar
1 oz (25g) mixed spice	1 cooking apple, grated
1 oz (25g) cinnamon	1 carrot, grated
1 tsp ground ginger	³/₄ pt (425ml) milk

Method:

1   Mix dry ingredients and add carrot and apple.
2   Add milk and mix well to make a stiff dough.
3   See below for cooking instructions.

M. Barr, Coatbridge

Clootie Duff

4 cups S. R. flour	1¹/₂ cups sugar
¹/₂ tsp salt	3 cups dried fruit
1 level tsp mixed spice	1 egg, beaten
1 level tsp cinnamon	1 tblsp syrup
¹/₂ level tsp ginger	1 tblsp treacle
¹/₂ level tsp nutmeg	1 apple, grated
6 oz (175g) margarine	¹/₂ tsp bicarbonate of soda
	milk to mix

Method:

1   Mix flour, salt and spices and rub in margarine.
2   Add sugar and dried fruit.
3   Mix egg, syrup, treacle and apple with a little milk.
4   Add to dry mixture and fold in bicarbonate of soda mixed in a little milk.
5   Mix to a dropping consistency, using more milk if required.
6   See below for cooking instructions.

A. Hughson, Stornoway, Lewis

To cook all the clootie dumplings:

1   Scald the "cloot" briefly in the pan of boiling water.
2   Ring out and dredge well with flour.
3   Turn mixture onto the cloth, tie up securely, making sure there are no loose edges and leaving room for the dumpling to swell.
4   Place dumpling on plate in pan of boiling water and boil for 3¹/₂-4 hours, topping up with boiling water if the level drops.
5   Lift dumpling onto a plate and carefully begin to remove the cloth, using the back of a knife to ensure the "skin" stays on the dumpling.
6   Invert dumpling onto a large plate and fully remove the cloth.
7   Leave dumpling to dry naturally,
8   Slice and eat hot or cold.

Cranberry Cheesecake

Base:
2 oz (50g) butter
4 oz (100g) digestive biscuits,
    crushed
1 tsp ground ginger

Filling:
1 tblsp gelatine
3 oz (75g) caster sugar
6 oz (175g) cream cheese
$^1/_2$ pt (300ml) double cream
1 small jar cranberry sauce

Topping:
1 small jar cranberry sauce
$^1/_4$ pt (150ml) double cream, whipped

Method:

1 Melt butter and add biscuits and ginger.
2 Press mixture into a deep 7" tin or flan dish and chill.
3 Dissolve gelatine in 4 tblsp hot water, leave for 10 minutes and then add the sugar.
4 Soften the cheese in a bowl and add the gelatine and sugar.
5 Lightly whip the cream, fold into mixture along with cranberry sauce.
6 Pour over biscuit base and chill for 1 hour.
7 Top with second jar of sauce and decorate with cream.

Effie Lamont, Glenelg

Orange Cheesecake

Base:
1 $^1/_2$ oz (40g) margarine
1 $^1/_2$ oz (40g) sugar
4 oz (100g) digestive biscuits,
    crushed

Filling:
1 tin mandarin oranges
1 orange jelly
6 oz (175g) Philadelphia cream cheese
$^1/_4$ pt (150ml) double cream, whipped

Method:

1 Melt margarine and add sugar and biscuits.
2 Press mixture into an 8" tin or flan dish and chill.
3 Drain juice from mandarins and make up to $^1/_2$ pint with water.
4 Heat the juice and dissolve the jelly in it.
5 Leave in the fridge until it begins to set.
6 Soften the cheese and beat into the jelly with whipped cream.
7 Break most of the mandarin oranges and add to mixture.
8 Pour over biscuit base and return to fridge to set.
9 Decorate with remaining mandarin oranges.

Ann Davis, Tarbat, Portmahomack

Rhubarb and Ginger Cheesecake (Cooked)

Base:

4 oz (100g) digestive biscuits
   crushed
2 oz (50g) margarine, melted
$^1/2$ tsp ground ginger

Topping:

$^1/4$ pt (150ml) soured cream
1 oz (25g) caster sugar

Filling:

8 oz (225g) rhubarb, chopped
2 pieces stem ginger, chopped
1 oz (25g) granulated sugar
1 tblsp ginger syrup
8 oz (225g) cream cheese
$^1/4$ pt (150ml) plain yoghurt
2 eggs, separated
2 oz (50g) soft brown sugar
1 oz (25g) plain flour

Method:

1   Melt margarine, add biscuits and ground ginger.
2   Press into an 8" loose-based cake tin and chill.
3   Put rhubarb, ginger, sugar and syrup in a pan and cook until the fruit is tender.
4   Cool and spoon over base.
5   Blend together cheese, yoghurt, egg yolks, brown sugar and flour and beat well.
6   Whisk the egg whites until stiff, fold into the cheese mixture and pour over the rhubarb.
7   Cook in a pre-heated oven 180°C/350°F/Gas 4 for 40-50 minutes or until firm and beginning to brown.
8   Mix the soured cream with the caster sugar and pour over the cheesecake.
9   Return to the oven for a further 10 minutes.
     Allow to cool before removing from tin.
     (Note: $^1/2$-$^3/4$ oz chopped ginger, 1 tblsp golden syrup and $^1/4$ tsp ground ginger may
          be substituted for the stem ginger and ginger syrup.)

Christine MacKenzie, Wick

Rhubarb Whip

1 lb (450g) rhubarb, cut in 1" pieces
$^1/4$ pt (150ml) water
4 oz (100g) granulated sugar

1 raspberry jelly
7 oz (200g) tin evaporated milk

Method:

1 Cook rhubarb in pan with water and sugar until really soft.
2 Cut the jelly into the hot rhubarb and stir until it melts.
3 Whip the evaporated milk until stiff and fold into the cooled rhubarb mixture.
4 Serve in a large glass bowl or individual dishes.

H. MacLean, Glenshiel

Rhubarb Torte

Base:

4 oz (100g) plain flour
^{1}/4 tsp salt
2 tblsp sugar
2 oz (50g) soft margarine

Meringue:

3 egg whites
2 oz (50g) caster sugar

Topping:

8 oz (200g) caster sugar
2 tblsp plain flour
3 egg yolks
3 fl oz cream or
    evaporated milk
2 ^{1}/4 cups rhubarb, chopped

Method:

1 Rub margarine into other "base" ingredients to make crumble and press into an
   8" x 8" tin.
2 Bake in a pre-heated oven 180°C/350°F/Gas 4 for 25 minutes.
3 Combine all "topping" ingredients in a pan and cook, stirring well, until clear.
4 Cool and pour over base.
5 Beat egg whites until stiff and fold in sugar.
6 Cover torte with meringue mixture and brown in oven, 220°C/425°F/Gas 7 for 5-10
   minutes.

Joyce MacFadzean, Cape Traverse, P.E.I.

Banana Split Cake

Base:

4 oz (100g) margarine
2 cups digestive biscuits, crushed

Topping:

1 tin crushed pineapple
2 or 3 bananas, sliced
^{1}/4 pt (150ml) double cream, whipped
grated chocolate to decorate

Filling:

2 cups icing sugar
2 oz (50g) butter, softened
2 eggs, well beaten

Method:

1 Melt margarine, add biscuits and press into a 9" tin or dish.
2 Whisk together icing sugar, butter and eggs until fluffy.
3 Cover the biscuit base with this mixture and chill.
4 Drain pineapple and spread over the filling.
5 Cover with sliced bananas and top with whipped cream.
6 Chill for 3-4 hours and decorate with grated chocolate.

Annie Graham, Oban

Raspberry Rhapsody

4 oz (100g) digestive biscuits, crushed
6 level tblsp drinking chocolate
3 oz (75g) demerara sugar
$^1/4$ pt (150ml) single cream
$^1/2$ pt (300ml) double cream
1 lb (450g) raspberries
grated chocolate to decorate

Method:

1   Mix biscuits, drinking chocolate and sugar.
2   Whip creams together until thick.
3   Spread a layer of cream on base of glass dish.
4   Scatter half the raspberries on top and cover with biscuit mixture.
5   Layer again, ending with cream and chill, preferably overnight.
6   Decorate with grated chocolate and a few raspberries.

K. Sutherland, Dingwall

Black Forest Gateau

4 eggs
4 oz (100g) caster sugar
3 oz (75g) S. R. flour
1 oz (25g) cocoa powder
$^1/2$ level tsp baking powder

2 sm tins black cherries, in syrup
1 tblsp cider or wine vinegar
$^1/2$ pt (300ml) whipping cream,
   whipped
grated chocolate

Method:

1   Whisk eggs and sugar together until light and fluffy.
2   Sieve flour, cocoa and baking powder into mixture.
3   Pour into 2 greased and floured 8" sandwich tins.
4   Bake in a pre-heated oven 180°C/350°F/Gas 4 for 20 minutes.
5   Drain cherries and add vinegar to the juice. (This is the secret ingredient which makes it taste special).
6   Place sponges on plates, soak in juice and leave to cool.
7   Layer cherries on base sponge and cover with half the cream.
8   Carefully lift the other sponge and place on top.
9   Cover with remaining cream and decorate with grated chocolate.

Julia Grier, Somerton Road, E.P.C. N. Ireland

Norwegian Apple Cake

4 large Bramley apples,
  peeled and sliced
2 large eggs
9 oz (250g) sugar

4 oz (100g) butter
$1/4$ pt (150ml) top of milk
$6 1/2$ oz (160g) S. R. flour

Method:

1 Spread the apples in an 8" x 12" baking tin.
2 Whisk eggs and 8 oz of the sugar until thick.
3 Bring butter and milk to the boil.
4 Pour onto the eggs and sugar and fold in the flour.
5 Pour the mixture over the apples and sprinkle with the remaining caster sugar.
6 Bake in a pre–heated oven 200°C/400°F/Gas 6 for 25 minutes.
7 Can be enjoyed hot or cold.   *Nancie MacLeod, Cole Abbey, London*

Lemon Surprise

3 lemons, juice and rind
1 large tin condensed milk
3 eggs, separated

1 plain sponge
$1/4$ pt (150ml) double cream
grated chocolate to decorate

Method:

1 Put grated rind and juice of lemon into a large bowl.
2 Add condensed milk and eggs yolks and mix well.
3 Whisk egg whites until stiff and fold gently into mixture.
4 Cover the base of a trifle dish with a layer of the mixture.
5 Add a layer of sponge and cover with more mixture.
6 Repeat and complete with a thick layer of lemon mixture.
7 Chill for at least 3 hours - preferably overnight.
8 Cover with whipped cream and a grating of chocolate.   *Pam Wood, Bishopbriggs*

Boodle's Orange Fool

6 trifle sponges, cut to size
2 oz sugar

grated rind and juice of
  2 oranges and 1 lemon
$1/2$ pt (300ml) double cream

Method

1 Line base and half way up the sides of deep dish with sponges.
2 Dissolve sugar in rind and juice of fruit.
3 Whip cream until beginning to thicken and add fruit mixture.
4 Pour mixture over sponge and chill for at least 2 hours.
5 Serve decorated with orange segments.   *Frances Connan, Cole Abbey, London*

Cranachan

4 tblsp coarse oatmeal
1/2 pt (300ml) whipping cream
2 tblsp caster sugar

1 tsp whisky liqueur or
   vanilla essence
fresh and frozen raspberries

Method:

1 Toast the oatmeal and allow to cool.
2 Whip the cream with the liqueur and sugar until thick, but not stiff.
3 Fold in almost all the toasted oatmeal.
4 Place raspberries in glasses and spoon over cream mixture.
5 Sprinkle with remaining oatmeal.

Isobel MacArthur, Callanish, Lewis

Custard Ice Cream

3 eggs
1 1/2 oz (40g) caster sugar
1 1/4 pt (750ml) milk

14 oz (400g) tin condensed milk
few drops vanilla essence

Method

1 Beat the eggs and sugar.
2 Scald the milk and stir a little into the eggs and sugar.
3 Mix well and then add the rest of the milk.
4 Return mixture to pan and cook slowly, stirring until it coats the back of the wooden spoon.
5 Remove from heat and stir in the condensed milk and essence.
6 Pour into a 3^1/2 pint container, cool and freeze.
7 Allow to soften before serving with fresh fruit salad.

Andrea Murray, Partick Highland, Glasgow

Strawberry Ice Cream

8 oz (225g) caster sugar
juice of 1 lemon
1 lb (450g) strawberries (frozen will do)
4 oz (100g) double cream

Method:

1 Melt sugar and lemon juice together.
2 Sieve (or liquidise) strawberries and add to sugar and juice
3 Beat cream until firm and fold into mixture.
4 Beat again, put into container and freeze.
5 Remove from freezer 10 minutes before serving.

Nan MacRae, Knockbain

Tiramisu

16-20 sponge fingers
4 tblsp rum (or to taste)
2 tblsp brandy (optional)
4 fl oz (100ml) strong black coffee

14 oz (400g) mascarpone
   (Italian cream cheese)
2 eggs, separated
4 tblsp icing sugar
grated plain chocolate

Method:

1 Layer sponge fingers in shallow bowl.
2 Mix 2 tblsp rum with brandy and coffee mixture and trickle over sponges.
3 Beat together cheese, egg yolks and icing sugar then add remaining rum.
4 Whisk egg whites until stiff (but not dry) and fold into cheese mixture.
5 Spoon over sponge fingers and sprinkle with chocolate.
6 Refrigerate overnight before serving.
   (Note: 11 oz (300g) cream cheese mixed with $^1/_4$ pt (150ml) double cream may be
      used in place of mascarpone.)

Fiona Beveridge, Wick

Quick Banoffi Pie

Base:

12 digestive biscuits
3 oz (75g) margarine, melted

Filling:

1 large tin condensed milk
2 oz (50g) margarine
2 tblsp syrup

Topping:

2 bananas, sliced
$^1/_4$ pt (150ml) double cream, whipped

Method:

1 Base –   Put biscuits into bowl, add melted margarine and mix.
             Press into a large flan dish and chill.
2 Filling – Put all ingredients into pan and melt slowly.
             Bring to caramelising point, stirring constantly.
             Pour over base and leave to cool completely.
3 Topping – Lay bananas on top of filling and cover with cream.

Alison Paterson, Golspie

Peach Delight

1 carton peach melba yoghurt
1 carton double cream

sliced tinned peaches
2 tblsp demerara sugar

Method:

1 Beat yoghurt and cream together.
2 Add drained, chopped peach slices and mix well.
3 Pour into serving dish and sprinkle with sugar.
4 Chill to allow sugar to permeate cream mixture.

P. Lyons, Stranmillis, E.P.C., N. Ireland

Lemon Cream

1 sachet gelatine

2 lemons, juice and rind

6 oz (175g) caster sugar

3 eggs, separated

$^1/_4$ pt (150ml) double cream

$^1/_4$ pt (150ml) single cream

Method:

1   Prepare sachet of gelatine as directed on packet.
2   Put grated rind and juice of lemon, sugar and egg yolks in pan and mix well.
3   Heat gently, but do not boil.
4   Stir in melted gelatine.
5   Beat creams together and add to cooled mixture before it sets.
6   Beat egg whites until very stiff and fold gently into mixture.
7   Chill for at least 2 hours and decorate as desired.   *Helen MacKay, St. Vincent St.-Milton, Glasgow*

Magic Lemon Pudding

2 oz (50g) margarine

4 oz (100g) caster sugar

2 eggs, separated

1 large lemon

2 oz (75g) S. R. flour

$^1/_2$ pt (300ml) milk

Method:

1   Cream margarine and sugar until light and fluffy
2   Beat in egg yolks and add juice and rind of lemon.
3   Gradually add flour and then milk.
4   Beat egg whites until stiff and fold into creamed mixture
5   Pour into a greased 1$^1/_2$ pint pie dish.
6   Stand dish in a roasting tin and add water to half way up.
7   Bake in a pre-heated oven 190°C/375°F/Gas 5 for 40-45 minutes.
8   May be served hot or cold.   *Margaret MacMillan, Partick Highland, Glasgow*

Chocolate Mould

$^1/_2$ pt (300ml) milk

1 tblsp gelatine

1 tblsp sugar

1 tblsp cocoa

2 eggs, separated

Method:

1   Put milk, gelatine, sugar and cocoa in a pan and heat gently until melted.
2   Add beaten egg yolks and stir until mixture thickens.
3   Beat egg whites very stiffly and fold into cooled and setting mixture.
4   Put in wetted mould to set, chill and serve.   *M. MacLeod, Barvas, Lewis*

Scones, Pancakes & Oatcakes

Oven Scones (1)

12 oz (350g) plain flour
pinch of salt
1 tsp cream of tartar
$^1/_2$ tsp bicarbonate of soda

2 dsp sugar
2 oz (50g) margarine
1 egg
milk

Method:

1 Mix dry ingredients together in a bowl.
2 Rub in margarine to resemble breadcrumbs.
3 Add egg and sufficient milk to make a soft dough.
4 Knead and roll out on a floured board to $^1/_4$" thickness.
5 Cut with 2" cutter and place on baking tray.
6 Bake in a pre-heated oven 230°C/450°F/Gas 8 for 8-10 minutes.
   (Note: For fruit scones add 2 oz (50g) sultanas.)

G. Bremner, Wick

Oven Scones (2)

1 lb (450g) S. R. flour
4 oz (100g) margarine
1 dsp granulated sugar

2 tblsp treacle
1 egg
milk

Method:

1 Rub margarine into flour to resemble breadcrumbs.
2 Mix in sugar, treacle and egg.
3 Add sufficient milk to make an elastic dough.
4 Knead and roll out on a floured board to $^1/_2$" thickness.
5 Cut with 2" cutter and place on baking tray.
6 Bake in a pre-heated oven 200°C/400°F/Gas 6 for 10-12 minutes.

Joan MacCallum, Campbeltown

Glencampa Scones

1 lb (450g) S. R. flour
1 tsp baking powder
4 oz (100g) margarine
2 eggs

4 tblsp treacle
2 tblsp syrup
milk
2 oz (50g) raisins

Method:

1 Rub margarine into dry ingredients to resemble breadcrumbs.
2 Beat eggs with treacle and syrup in a little milk.
3 Add to mixture along with raisins to form a stiff dough.
4 Knead and roll out on a floured board to $^1/_4$" thickness.
5 Cut with 2" cutter and place on a baking tray.
6 Bake in a pre-heated oven 230°C/450°F/Gas 8 for 10-15 minutes.

J. M. Morrison, Carloway, Lewis

Treacle Scones

1 lb (450g) plain flour
1 tsp bicarbonate of soda
2 tsp cream of tartar
1 tsp ginger
1 tsp cinnamon

4 oz (100g) butter
2 tsp treacle
milk

Method:

1 Sift flour and add all dry ingredients.
2 Rub in butter to resemble breadcrumbs.
3 Melt treacle and milk in pan.
4 Add to mixture to form a soft dough.
5 Roll out on a floured board, cut into rounds or triangles and place on a baking tray.
6 Bake in a pre-heated oven 230°C/450°F/Gas 8 for 12 minutes. *Catherine MacIver, Point, Lewis*

Wholemeal Scones

4 oz (100g) plain flour
4 oz (100g) wholemeal flour
$^1/_2$ tsp salt
2 tsp baking powder
$^1/_2$ tsp cinnamon

1 oz (25g) caster sugar
1 oz (25g) butter
2 oz (50g) dates, chopped
$^1/_4$ pt (150ml) milk

Method:

1 Sift the flours into a bowl and add all dry ingredients.
2 Rub in butter to resemble breadcrumbs and then add dates.
3 Add sufficient milk to form a soft dough ($^1/_4$ pt less 1 tblsp).
4 Knead and roll out on a floured board to $^3/_4$" thickness.
5 Cut with a 2" cutter and place on a baking tray.
6 Bake in a pre-heated oven 230°C/450°F/Gas 8 for 10-12 minutes. *C. Reid, Lochs, Lewis*

Cheese Oatmeal Scones

4 oz (100g) plain flour	1 oz (25g) margarine/lard
1/2 tsp bicarbonate of soda	4 oz oatmeal
1 tsp cream of tartar	2 oz (50g) cheese, grated
1/2 tsp salt	a little milk

Method:

1 Sift flour, bicarbonate of soda, cream of tartar and salt into a bowl.
2 Rub in margarine (or lard) to resemble breadcrumbs.
3 Add oatmeal and cheese and mix well.
4 Add sufficient milk to form a stiff dough.
5 Knead lightly and roll out quite thickly on a floured board.
6 Cut into rounds and place on greased baking tray.
7 Bake in a pre-heated oven 230°C/450°F/Gas 8 for 12 minutes.

C. Smith, Point, Lewis

Girdle Scones

8 oz (225g) plain flour	1 oz (25g) margarine
1 oz (25g) caster sugar	1/4 pt (150ml) water
1 tsp bicarbonate of soda	
2 tsp cream of tartar	
2 tblsp dried milk	

Method:

1 Heat the girdle.
2 Mix all the dry ingredients and rub in margarine.
3 Mix with water to a fairly stiff dough.
4 Roll out on a floured board into a round approx. 9"-10".
5 Cut into 4 sections and transfer to girdle.
6 Bake and turn to do second side when under side is cooked.

Marietta MacDonald, Carloway, Lewis

Potato Scones

8 oz (225g) cooked potatoes
2 oz (50g) plain flour or oatmeal
pinch of salt

Method:

1 Mash potatoes very smoothly.
2 Put flour, salt and potatoes on a baking board.
3 Work in as much flour as potatoes will take up. (Less flour will be required if potatoes are very dry).
4 Roll out very thinly and cut into rounds.
5 Place on a hot girdle and prick all over with fork.
6 Cook for 2-3 minutes on either side.
7 Cool between a folded tea-towel.

Anon, Nairn, Croy & Ardersier

Pancakes (1)

10 oz (275g) S. R. flour
2 oz (50g) caster sugar
1 level tsp bicarbonate of soda
1 level tsp cream of tartar
pinch of salt

1 egg
1 tblsp syrup
1/4 pt (150ml) milk

Method:

1   Grease girdle with a knob of margarine and pre-heat.
2   Sieve all dry ingredients into a bowl.
3   Add egg, syrup and milk. (A little extra milk may be needed to reach dropping consistency).
4   Bake spoonfuls of mixture immediately on prepared girdle, turning pancake to do under side.

Christine Stone, Castletown

Pancakes (2)

8 oz (225g) S. R. flour
3 oz (75g) caster sugar
3/4 level tsp bicarbonate of soda
1 1/2 level tsp cream of tartar
pinch of salt

2 eggs (size 3)
1 dsp syrup
2 tsp cooking oil
8 tblsp milk

Method:

1   Grease girdle (or non-stick pan) and pre-heat.
2   Sieve all dry ingredients into a bowl.
3   Add eggs, syrup, oil and milk and beat well.
4   Bake dessert spoons of mixture on prepared girdle, turning pancake to do under side.
5   Cool between a folded tea-towel to prevent drying out.
    (Note: For a lighter pancake, use 6 tblsp milk and 2 tblsp water.)

Isbbel Cameron, Kyle

Butteries

1 3/4 lb (800g) bread flour
1/2 oz (15g) sugar
3/4 oz (20g) salt
1 1/2 oz (40g) fat

2 oz (50g) yeast
3/4 pt (425ml) water
12 oz (350g) butter

Method:

1   Rub fat into sieved dry ingredients in a bowl.
2   Mix yeast and water and add to dry ingredients to make dough.
3   Prove dough, leaving covered for 1 hour.
4   Chop butter into dough and then divide into 1 1/2 oz pieces.
5   Leave covered, on a baking tray, for 20 minutes.
6   Bake in a pre-heated oven 230°C/450°F/Gas 8 for 10-12 minutes.

Sheila Grant, Cumbernauld

Wholemeal Bread

8 oz (225g) S. R. flour
8 oz (225g) wholemeal flour
1 tsp salt
1 tsp baking powder
1 tsp bicarbonate of soda
1 tsp cream of tartar

2 oz (50g) butter
1 tblsp syrup
1 egg, beaten
1/2 pt (300ml) milk
1 tblsp oats

Method:

1   Mix all the dry ingredients (except oats) in a large bowl.
2   Rub in butter to resemble breadcrumbs.
3   Add syrup, egg and milk to form a soft dough.
4   Place in a greased 2 lb loaf tin and sprinkle with oats.
5   Bake in a pre-heated oven 190°C/375°F/Gas 5 for 40-45 minutes

Christine Lamont, Snizort, Skye

Oatcakes (1)

9 oz (250g) oatmeal
3 oz (75g) S. R. flour
1/2 tsp bicarbonate of soda
1/2 tsp cream of tartar
1/4 tsp salt

2 oz (50g) melted butter
milk to mix

Method:

1   Put dry ingredients into a bowl.
2   Add melted butter and sufficient milk to make a pliable dough.
3   Roll out in oatmeal and cut as desired.
4   Bake in a pre-heated oven 180°C/350°F/Gas 4 for 30-35 minutes.

C. Ross, Lochcarron

Oatcakes (2)

8 oz (225g) oatmeal
4 oz (100g) wholemeal flour
pinch of bicarbonate of soda
pinch of salt

3 oz (75g) lard
4 fl oz (120ml) hot water

Method:

1   Put dry ingredients into a bowl.
2   Melt lard in hot water and allow to cool.
3   Add to dry ingredients to make a pliable dough.
4   Roll out in flour and cut as desired.
5   Bake in a pre-heated oven 160°C/325°F/Gas 3 for 40 minutes.

Annie MacDonald, Dunvegan, Skye

Tea Loaves

Fruit Loaf (1)

8 fl oz (240ml) water
4 oz (100g) margarine
4 oz (100g) sugar
8 oz (225g) dried fruit
1 tsp mixed spice
1 tsp bicarbonate of soda

2 eggs, beaten
8 oz (225g) S. R. flour

Method:

1　Simmer all ingredients (except eggs and flour) in pan for 5 minutes.
2　Remove from heat and leave to cool.
3　Add beaten eggs and flour and mix well.
4　Spoon mixture into a greased and base-lined 2 lb loaf tin.
5　Bake in a pre-heated oven 180°C/350°F/Gas 4 for 1¼ hours.

Maisie Robertson, Dunoon

Fruit Loaf (2)

2 cups raisins
2 cups sultanas
2 cups sugar
2 cups water
2 eggs, well-beaten

6 oz (175g) margarine
1 lb (450g) plain flour
2 tsp bicarbonate of soda
1 tsp ginger
1 tsp cinnamon
1 tsp mixed spice

Method:

1　Put raisins, sultanas, sugar and water in pan, bring to the boil, simmer for 2-3 minutes and allow to cool.
2　Add eggs to cooled mixture and stir well.
3　Rub margarine into flour and add dry ingredients.
4　Add "moist" mixture to "dry" mixture and mix well.
5　Spoon mixture into 2 greased and base-lined 2 lb loaf tins.
6　Bake in a pre-heated oven 180°C/350°F/Gas 4 for 1-1½ hours.

J. D. MacKirdy, Rothesay

 **Tea Loaves**

Tea Loaf

4 oz (100g) margarine
6 oz (175g) dried fruit
4 oz (100g) sugar
$^1/_2$ pt (300ml) tea

9 oz (250g) S. R. flour
1 tsp bicarbonate of soda
1 tsp mixed spice

Method:

1 Put margarine, fruit, sugar and tea in a pan.
2 Bring slowly to boil, simmer for 5 minutes and allow to cool.
3 Add sieved flour, bicarbonate of soda and spice to cooled mixture.
4 Spoon mixture into a greased and base-lined 2 lb loaf tin.
5 Bake in a pre-heated oven 180°C/350°F/Gas 4 for 1-1$^1/_4$ hours.

Ruth Burke, Knock E.P.C., N. Ireland

Raisin Riser

6 oz (175g) California raisins ·
2 oz (50g) All-bran
3 oz (75g) demerara sugar
$^1/_2$ pt (300ml) milk

1 egg, beaten
6 oz (175g) S. R. flour
2 tblsp apricot jam

Method:

1 Put raisins, All-bran, sugar and milk in a bowl and leave covered for 1 hour.
2 Stir egg and sifted flour into raisin mixture.
3 Spoon mixture into a greased and base-lined 2 lb loaf tin.
4 Bake in a pre-heated oven 190°C/375°F/Gas 5 for 1 $^1/_4$ hours.
5 Leave to cool for 5 minutes.
6 Melt apricot jam and brush over warm loaf if desired.

Lucy Ross, Melvich

Weetabix Loaf

3 Weetabix, crushed
8 oz (225g) soft brown sugar
6 oz (175g) sultanas
$^1/_2$ pt (300ml) milk

$^1/_4$ tsp ground ginger
$^1/_4$ tsp ground cloves
$^1/_2$ tsp salt
7 oz (200g) S. R. flour
2 eggs, well beaten

Method:

1 Soak all ingredients (except flour and eggs) overnight.
2 Add flour and eggs and beat well.
3 Spoon mixture into a greased and base-lined 2 lb loaf tin.
4 Bake in a pre-heated oven 190°C/375°F/Gas 5 for 1-1$^1/_2$ hours.

M. Davis, Dumbarton

Yoghurt Loaf

1 small carton yoghurt (plain or flavoured)
(Wash out carton and use as a measure)

2 cartons caster sugar
3 cartons S.R. flour
5 oz (150g) melted margarine
2 eggs, beaten

Method:

1   Mix all ingredients thoroughly.
2   Spoon mixture into 2 greased and base-lined 1 lb loaf tins.
3   Bake in a pre-heated oven 180°C/350°F/Gas 4 for $^3/_4$–1 hour.

M. Buchanan, Kilwinning

Smiddy Dumpling

1 cup water
1 cup caster sugar
12 oz (350g) sultanas
1 tsp mixed spice
1 tsp bicarbonate of soda
4 oz (100g) margarine
1 carrot, finely grated

1 cup S.R. flour
1 cup plain flour
2 eggs, well-beaten

Method:

1   Put water, sugar, sultanas, spice, bicarbonate of soda, margarine and carrot into a pan.
2   Bring to the boil, simmer for 2 minutes and allow to cool.
3   Add flours and eggs to cooled mixture and mix well.
4   Spoon mixture into a greased and base-lined 2 lb loaf tin.
5   Bake in a pre-heated oven 150°C/300°F/Gas 3 for 1–1$^1/_2$ hours.

Katy-Ann Forteith, Oban

Lemon Loaf

4 oz (100g) margarine
5 oz (150g) caster sugar
1 egg
$^1/_2$ cup milk
8 oz (225g) S. R. flour
grated rind of $^1/_2$ lemon

Topping:
Mix together juice of
$^1/_2$ lemon and 2 tblsp
caster sugar

Method:

1   Cream margarine with sugar.
2   Beat egg and milk together.
3   Add flour and lemon rind alternately with egg and milk into the creamed mixture.
4   Spoon mixture into a greased and base-lined 2 lb loaf tin.
5   Bake in a pre-heated oven 190°C/375°F/Gas 5 for under 1 hour.
6   Pour topping mixture over hot loaf in tin and leave to cool.

Irene Howat, Campbeltown

 *Tea Loaves*

Banana and Walnut Loaf

4 oz (100g) butter
6 oz (175g) caster sugar
2 large eggs, beaten
3 bananas, mashed

3 oz (75g) walnuts, chopped
8 oz (225g) S. R. flour
$^1/_2$ tsp salt

Method:

1   Cream butter and sugar, add eggs and bananas and mix well.
2   Add walnuts and fold in flour with salt.
3   Spoon mixture into a greased and base-lined 2 lb loaf tin.
4   Bake in a pre-heated oven 160°C/325°F/Gas 3 for 1 $^1/_4$ hours.

Audrey Craig, Crumlin E.P.C., N. Ireland

Date and Walnut Loaf

8 oz (225g) dates, chopped
4 oz (100g) sugar
2 oz (50g) margarine
1 level tsp bicarbonate of soda
pinch of salt
$^1/_4$ pt (150ml) boiling water

8 oz (225g) S. R. flour
2 oz (50g) walnuts, chopped
1 egg, beaten
1 tsp vanilla essence

Method:

1   Put dates, sugar, margarine, bicarbonate of soda and salt in a bowl.
2   Pour over the boiling water and mix well to melt margarine.
3   Add remaining ingredients and mix again.
4   Spoon mixture into a greased and base-lined 2 lb (or 2 x 1lb) loaf tin.
5   Bake in a pre-heated oven 160°C/325°F/Gas 3 for 1-1$^1/_4$ hours.   *Joyce MacRae, Glenshiel*

Date and Orange Loaf

8 oz (225g) pkt sugared dates
4 fl oz (120ml) water
8 oz (225g) soft brown sugar
3 oz (75g) margarine
2 tblsp orange juice
grated rind of 1 orange

1 egg, beaten
8 oz (225g) S. R. flour
1 tsp cinnamon

Method:

1   Simmer dates and water gently in a pan until dates are pulpy.
2   Add sugar and stir until dissolved.
3   Remove from heat, add margarine and mix well.
4   Add juice and rind from orange and leave to cool.
5   Gradually add egg with sieved flour and cinnamon to mixture.
6   Spoon mixture into a greased and base-lined 2 lb loaf tin.
7   Bake in a pre-heated oven 180°C/350°F/Gas 4 for 1 $^1/_4$ hours.   *Mary Marquis, Tarbert, Argyll*

Sticky Gingerbread (1)

6 oz (175g) margarine
9 oz (250g) treacle
3 oz (75g) syrup
3 oz (75g) soft brown sugar
8 fl oz (240ml) milk

12 oz (350g) plain flour
2 level tsp ground ginger
1 rounded tsp mixed spice
1 rounded tsp bicarbonate of soda
3 eggs, beaten
2 oz (50g) raisins

Method:

1 Warm margarine, treacle, syrup and sugar in a pan.
2 Add milk and allow to cool.
3 Sieve the dry ingredients into a bowl.
4 Add the treacle mixture, the eggs and raisins and beat well.
5 Spoon mixture into a lined 2 lb loaf tin.
6 Bake in a pre-heated oven 150°C/300°F/Gas 2 for 2 hours or until firm to touch.

Elizabeth MacKay, Bishopbriggs

Sticky Gingerbread (2)

8 oz (225g) margarine
8 oz (225g) treacle
8 oz (225g) soft brown sugar
^{1}/2 pt (300ml) milk, warmed
2 level tsp bicarbonate of soda

12 oz (350g) plain flour
2 level dsp ginger
3 level dsp cinnamon
2 eggs, beaten

Method:

1 Melt margarine, treacle and sugar in a pan.
2 Pour warmed milk over bicarbonate of soda in a jug.
3 Sieve the dry ingredients into a bowl and add milk and eggs.
4 Add melted ingredients and mix well.
5 Spoon mixture into a lined 7 ^{1}/2" x 11 ^{1}/2" tin.
6 Bake in a pre-heated oven 180°C/350°F/Gas 4 for 1^1/2 hours, covering with greaseproof paper after ^{1}/2 hour.

E. A. MacRae, Lochcarron

Fail - Me - Never Gingerbread

4 oz (100g) margarine
1 cup sugar
2 eggs, well beaten
1 tblsp syrup
1 tblsp treacle

2 cups plain flour
1 tsp mixed spice
1 tsp ground ginger
1 tsp bicarbonate of soda
1 cup hot water

Method:

1 Cream margarine and sugar, add eggs and beat well.
2 Add syrup and treacle to creamed mixture.
3 Mix together flour and spices and fold them into mixture.
4 Mix bic. of soda with water and add to the mixture.
5 Spoon into a greased and base-lined 2 lb loaf tin.
6 Bake in a pre-heated oven 180°C/350°F/Gas 4 for 1 hour.

Mary Boyd, Lochgilphead

Bran Muffins

Dry Mixture:

1 $^1/_4$ cups S. R. flour
1 tsp baking powder
$^1/_2$ tsp salt

Moist Mixture:

1 $^1/_2$ cups All-Bran cereal
1 $^1/_4$ cups milk
1 egg, lightly beaten
$^3/_4$ cup vegetable oil
$^1/_2$ cup honey

Method:

1 Stir dry mixture together in a bowl.
2 Steep All-Bran and milk in a small bowl until well combined.
3 Add egg to oil and honey and stir into bran and milk mixture.
4 Add moist mixture to dry mixture all at once and stir until blended, but still lumpy.
5 Fill greased muffin cups $^3/_4$ full.
6 Bake in a pre-heated oven 200°C/400°F/Gas 6 for 20-25 minutes or until brown and springy to touch.

K. Macaskill, Carloway, Lewis

Boiled Raisin Muffins

$^1/_2$ cup raisins
1 $^1/_2$ cups water
$^1/_2$ cup margarine
$^2/_3$ cup brown sugar
1 egg
1 tsp vanilla essence

1 $^1/_2$ cups plain flour
1 tsp baking powder
1 tsp bicarbonate of soda
$^1/_4$ tsp salt

Method:

1 Simmer raisins in water in a covered pan for 20 minutes.
2 Cream margarine and sugar and beat in egg and essence.
3 Add raisin mixture, sift in dry ingredients and mix well.
4 Spoon mixture into greased muffin cups.
5 Bake in a pre-heated oven 180°C/350°F/Gas 4 for 15-20 minutes.

M. Gunn, Lochs, Lewis

Cakes

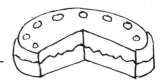

Chocolate Sponge

6 oz (175g) margarine
6 oz (175g) sugar
5 oz (150g) S. R. flour, sieved

3 eggs
1 oz (25g) cocoa
1 $^1/_2$ tsp baking powder

Method:

1 Cream margarine and sugar.
2 Add flour and eggs alternately, beating mixture in between.
3 Add cocoa and baking powder and beat thoroughly for 3-4 minutes.
4 Put mixture into a greased and floured deep 7"-8" tin and bake in a pre-heated oven 200°C/400°F/Gas 6 for approx. 25 minutes.
5 Cool in tin before turning out on to a wire tray.
6 Decorate with chocolate or coffee butter icing or fresh cream sprinkled with nuts.

Moreen Moller, Tarbert, Argyll

Milk Chocolate Sponge

7 oz (200g) S. R. flour
8 oz (225g) caster sugar
$^1/_2$ tsp salt
1 oz (25g) cocoa

4 oz (100g) margarine
2 eggs, beaten
5 tsp evaporated milk
5 tblsp hot water
a few drops vanilla essence

Method:

1 Sieve flour, sugar, salt and cocoa into a bowl and rub in margarine.
2 Beat eggs with milk, add water and essence and beat well.
3 Put mixture into two greased and floured 7" tins and bake in a pre-heated oven 180°C/350°F/Gas 4 for 30-35 minutes.
4 Sandwich together and cover with chocolate icing when cold.

Chocolate Icing:

2 $^1/_2$ oz (65g) margarine
1 tblsp cocoa
9 oz (250g) icing sugar, sieved

3 tblsp hot milk
1 tsp vanilla essence

Method:

1 Melt margarine and blend in cocoa.
2 Beat in sugar, milk and essence until smooth and thick.

Rene Stewart, St Columba, Edinburgh

 *Cakes*

All In One Victoria Sponge

6 oz (175g) S. R. flour
1 level tsp baking powder
6 oz (175g) soft margarine

3 eggs (size 3)
2 tblsp milk
6 oz (175g) caster sugar

Method:

1 Sieve flour with baking powder, add margarine, eggs, milk and sugar.
2 Beat with wooden spoon for 2-3 minutes or with electric beater for 1 minute.
3 Put mixture into 2 greased and floured 7" tins and bake in a pre-heated oven 180°C/350°F/Gas 4 for 35 minutes.
4 Cool and decorate with appropriate filling and covering.

J. Thomson, Paisley

Wholemeal Victoria Sandwich Sponge

6 oz (175g) soft margarine
6 oz (175g) caster sugar
3 eggs (size 3), separated

2 tblsp cold water
6 oz (175g) wholemeal S. R. flour
red jam
icing sugar to decorate

Method:

1 Cream margarine and sugar, beat in egg yolks and water.
2 Whisk egg whites to a light foam in a separate bowl.
3 Gently fold in flour, then egg whites into creamed mixture.
4 Put mixture into 2 greased and lined 7" tins and bake in a pre-heated oven 180°C/350°F/Gas 4 for 20-25 minutes.
5 Cool, sandwich with jam and dust with icing sugar.

B. Murray, Cross, Lewis

Spicy Sponge

5 oz (150g) caster sugar
5 oz (150g) margarine
3 eggs
1 tblsp syrup

5 oz (150g) S. R. flour
1 tsp mixed spice
$^1/_2$ tsp cinnamon
$^1/_2$ tsp ginger

Method:

1 Cream sugar and margarine, add eggs, one at a time.
2 Add a little flour if curdling, beat in syrup.
3 Sieve dry ingredients and gently fold in.
4 Put mixture into 2 greased and floured 7" tins and bake in a pre-heated oven 180°C/350°F/Gas 4 for 20-30 minutes.
5 Cool and sandwich together with desired filling.

Mary Black, Rosskeen

Egg Sponge

2 eggs (size 1), separated
4 oz (100g) caster sugar
2 tblsp hot water

3 oz (75g) S. R. flour
cream, whipped
icing sugar

Method:

1 Beat egg whites until stiff, add sugar and whip until soft peaks form.
2 Add egg yolks and whip until really milky.
3 Add water a little at a time, beating between each addition.
4 Fold in sifted flour and mix well.
5 Put mixture into 2 greased and lined 8" tins and bake in a pre-heated oven
   180°C/350°F/Gas 4 for 25 minutes.
6 Cool, sandwich together with cream and dust with icing sugar.   *I. Ross, Dornoch*

Country Fruit Cake

12 oz (350g) plain flour
3 level tsp baking powder
6 oz (175g) margarine
6 oz (175g) soft brown sugar
6 oz (175g) sultanas
6 oz (175g) currants

2 level tsp golden syrup
3 eggs (size 3)
1 rounded tblsp marmalade
3 rounded tblsp demerara sugar

Method:

1 Sift flour and baking powder into a bowl.
2 Add margarine and rub in until mixture resembles fine breadcrumbs.
3 Stir in soft brown sugar and fruit.
4 Place carefully measured syrup in a bowl, add eggs and marmalade, beat well and stir
   into dry ingredients.
5 Spoon mixture into a greased and lined 8" square tin.
6 Sprinkle the top with demerara sugar.
7 Bake in a pre-heated oven 150°C/300°F/Gas 2 for 2-2 1/4 hours.
8 Leave to cool in tin for 30 minutes, turn out and remove paper.   *A. Maclean, North Tolsta, Lewis*

Mincemeat Cake

5 oz (150g) margarine
5 oz (150g) caster sugar
2 eggs, beaten

8 oz (225g) S. R. flour
1 lb (450g) jar of mincemeat

Method:

1 Put all ingredients in a bowl and beat for 1-2 minutes until blended.
2 Spoon mixture into a lined 8" cake tin.
3 Bake in a pre-heated oven 160°C/325°F/Gas 3 for 1 3/4 hours.   *Isabel Bain, Tain*

Sultana Cake (1)

8 oz (225g) margarine
8 oz (225g) caster sugar
2 eggs, beaten

10 oz (275g) plain flour
1 tsp baking powder
a pinch of salt
1 small tin evaporated milk
1 lb (450g) sultanas or mixed fruit

Method:

1 Cream margarine and sugar and add eggs.
2 Add flour, baking powder, salt and milk and mix well.
3 Fold in fruit and mix well.
4 Spoon mixture into a deep greased and floured 8" cake tin.
5 Bake in a pre-heated oven 180°C/350°F/Gas 4 for 1 hour, then reduce to 160°C/325°F/Gas 3 for 1¹/₂ hours.

Anne Thomson, Drumchapel, Glasgow

Sultana Cake (2)

4 oz (100g) margarine
4 oz (100g) butter
8 oz (225g) caster sugar
4 large eggs, beaten

4 oz (100g) S. R. flour
6 oz (175g) plain flour
a pinch of salt
8 oz (225g) sultanas
4 tblsp milk

Method:

1 Beat margarine, butter and sugar to a cream.
2 Add eggs slowly along with some sifted flour and salt.
3 Beat mixture for a few minutes, add fruit along with some flour and mix thoroughly.
4 Add the rest of the flour and enough milk to make the mixture drop easily from the spoon.
5 Spoon mixture into a lined 8" cake tin, smooth the top and make a slight depression in the middle.
6 Bake in a pre-heated oven 180°C/350°F/Gas 4 for 30 minutes, then reduce to 160°C/325°F/Gas 3 for 1¹/₂ hours.
7 Leave in tin until cool before turning out.

Jenny MacDonald, Helmsdale

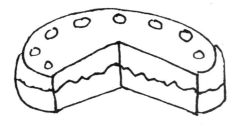

Orange Fruit Cake

9 oz (250g) margarine
8 oz (225g) caster sugar
3 eggs, beaten
5 oz (150g) S. R. flour
5 oz (150g) plain flour

rind of small orange
1 tblsp orange juice
1 tblsp thick marmalade
6 oz (175g) sultanas
6 oz (175g) glacé cherries, chopped

Method:

1 Cream margarine and sugar and add eggs with a little flour.
2 Add remaining flour, rind, juice and marmalade.
3 Fold in sultanas and cherries and mix carefully.
4 Spoon mixture into a greased and lined 10" cake tin.
5 Bake in centre of a pre-heated oven 160°C/325°F/Gas 3 for 1¹/₂ hours.
   (Note: Cover with foil if it browns too quickly.)

Annabel Robertson, Dundee

Almond Feather Cake

8 oz (225g) butter
8 oz (225g) caster sugar
a few drops almond essence

4 large eggs, beaten
5 oz (150g) S. R. flour
3 oz (75g) ground almonds.

Method:

1 Cream butter and sugar until pale and fluffy and add essence.
2 Beat in eggs gradually with a little flour.
3 Fold in sifted flour and ground almonds.
4 Spoon mixture into a greased and floured 8" square tin.
5 Bake in a pre-heated oven 180°C/350°F/Gas 4 for 1 hour.
   (Note: Top may be brushed with milk and sprinkled with caster sugar before going
      into the oven, or covered with a thin layer of glacé icing when cold.)

Anna Sutherland, C.W.I., Sydney

Lemon Cake

4 oz (100g) soft margarine
6 oz (175g) caster sugar
6 oz (175g) S. R. flour
4 tblsp milk

2 large eggs
rind and juice of 1 lemon
3 tblsp icing sugar

Method:

1 Beat together the margarine, caster sugar, flour, milk, eggs and rind.
2 Spoon mixture into a greased and lined 2 lb loaf tin.
3 Bake in a pre-heated oven 180°C/350°F/Gas 4 for 40 minutes.
4 Dissolve icing sugar in lemon juice over a low heat, pour over cake while still
   warm and leave to cool in tin.

E. Macleod, Lairg

Cinnamon Cake

4 oz (100g) butter
7 oz (200g) sugar
2 eggs
1/4 pt (150ml) soured cream
2 tsp vanilla essence

4 oz (100g) plain flour
2 tsp baking powder
a pinch of salt
5 oz (150g) walnuts or pecans, chopped
2 tsp ground cinnamon

Method:

1 Cream together butter and 6 oz (175g) of sugar.
2 Beat in the eggs, cream and essence.
3 Fold in flour, baking powder and salt, but do not over-beat.
4 Mix together remaining sugar, nuts and cinnamon.
5 Spoon half cake mixture into a greased and lined 8" cake tin.
6 Sprinkle over half the nut mixture, add the remaining cake mixture and top with remainder of nut mixture.
7 Bake in a pre-heated oven 180°C/350°F/Gas 4 for 35-40 minutes.
8 Serve hot or cold.

R. Finlay, Free North, Inverness

Banana Cake

4 oz (100g) margarine
8 oz (225g) S. R. flour
2 eggs, beaten
6 oz (175g) caster sugar

3 ripe bananas, mashed
6 oz (175g) sultanas
   or mixed fruit
1 oz (25g) walnuts, chopped
2 oz (50g) cherries, chopped

Method:

1 Rub margarine into flour.
2 Add rest of ingredients and mix well.
3 Spoon mixture into a greased and lined 8" cake tin.
4 Bake in a pre-heated oven 180°C/350°F/Gas 4 for 1 1/2 hours.

Ella Macdonald, Duirinish, Skye

Nut Cake

2 oz (50g) margarine
4 oz (100g) dark brown sugar
1 large egg

2 oz (50g) chopped walnuts
3 oz (75g) S. R. flour
4 oz (100g) sultanas

Method:

1 Melt margarine and sugar in pan - DO NOT BOIL.
2 Remove pan from heat, add egg and half of the nuts.
3 Sift in the flour and add fruit.
4 Spoon mixture into a greased 7" x 7" square tin and sprinkle top with remaining nuts before putting into oven.
5 Bake in a pre-heated oven 180°C/350°F/Gas 4 for 30 minutes.

Elsie Mackenzie, Tain

Eggless Spicy Apple Cake

4 oz (100g) butter or margarine
4 oz (100g) sugar
³/4 cup stewed apple, warmed
1 level tsp bicarbonate of soda

6 oz (175g) S.R. flour
1 level tsp cocoa
¹/4 level tsp nutmeg
¹/2 level tsp cinnamon
3 oz (75g) seedless raisins

Method:

1   Cream butter and sugar.
2   Mix soda into apple and add to creamed mixture.
3   Stir in flour, cocoa and spices mixed with the fruit.
4   Spoon mixture into a lined 7" cake tin.
5   Bake in a pre-heated oven 150°C/300°F/Gas 2 for 1 hour.
6   Remove from tin when cold, cover with glacé icing and dust with ground cinnamon.

E. M. E. Hood, Perth

Carrot Cake (1)

6 oz (175g) caster sugar
6 oz (175g) S. R. flour
¹/2 tsp baking powder
¹/2 tsp bicarbonate of soda
¹/2 tsp cinnamon
¹/2 tsp salt

2 eggs
8 fl oz (240ml) oil
4 oz (100g) carrots, grated
¹/2 of 14 oz (400g) tin crushed
   pineapple, well drained
2 oz (50g) walnuts, chopped
1 tblsp lemon juice

Method:

1   Mix together all dry ingredients, add eggs and oil and mix well.
2   Stir in carrots, pineapple, walnuts and lemon juice.
3   Spoon mixture into a greased and floured 8¹/2" cake tin.
4   Bake in a pre-heated oven 180°C/350°F/Gas 4 for approx 1 hour.

Topping:

6 oz (175g) icing sugar
1 oz (25g) butter

2 oz (50g) cream cheese
1 tsp vanilla essence

Method:

1   Cream together all ingredients.
2   Cover cold cake with topping and pat all over with the back of a teaspoon to give a peaked effect.

Olwen Ford, Coatbridge

 *Cakes*

Carrot Cake (2)

10 oz (275g) caster sugar
8 fl oz (240ml) sunflower seed oil
3 eggs
6 oz (175g) S. R. flour, sifted
1 $^1/_2$ tsp baking powder
1 $^1/_2$ tsp ground cinnamon

$^1/_2$ tsp ground cloves
$^1/_2$ tsp sea salt
8 oz (225g) carrots, finely grated
4 oz (100g) walnuts, finely chopped

Method:

1   Put sugar into a large bowl, stir in oil and beat with a wooden spoon.
2   Break in eggs one at a time, beating until each one is incorporated.
3   Gradually beat in flour, baking powder, cinnamon, cloves and salt.
4   Stir in carrots and nuts.
5   Spoon mixture into a greased and lined 7" or 8" round cake tin.
6   Bake in a pre-heated oven 180°C/350°F/Gas 4 for 70-80 minutes or until top jumps
    back when pressed with finger.
7   Cool on a wire rack.

Frosting:

3 oz (75g) cream cheese
1 $^1/_2$ oz (40g) unsalted butter, cut in small pieces
3 tblsp caster sugar

Method:

1   Beat cheese and butter together until smooth.
2   Add sugar and continue beating.
3   Spread frosting on top of cold cake, smoothing with a palette knife dipped in hot water.

Effie Lamont, Glenelg.

Pineapple Cake

6 oz (175g) soft brown sugar
4 oz (100g) soft margarine
12 oz (350g) mixed dried fruit
4 oz (100g) cherries (optional)

small tin crushed pineapple,
    drained
8 oz (225g) flour
2 eggs, beaten

Method:

1   Put sugar, margarine, dried fruit, cherries and pineapple into a pan.
2   Allow the mixture to melt over a low heat, stirring until it boils.
3   Remove from heat and allow to cool.
4   Add flour and eggs and blend well.
5   Spoon mixture into a greased and lined 8" cake tin.
6   Bake in a pre-heated oven 150°C/300°F/Gas 2 for 1 hour 40 minutes.

Mary Macleod, Bracadale, Skye

Boiled Fruit Cake (low-fat)

4 oz (100g) brown sugar

3 oz (75g) polyunsaturated margarine

1 lb mixed dried fruit

2 tsp mixed spice

1 tsp baking powder

1 pt (600ml) water

2 eggs, beaten

1 lb (450g) S.R. wholemeal flour

2 oz (50g) walnuts, chopped

Method:

1 Put all ingredients (except eggs, flour and walnuts) into a large pan.
2 Bring to the boil, reduce heat and simmer for 15 minutes.
3 Leave to cool for 30 minutes.
4 Beat in eggs and gradually stir in flour and walnuts.
5 Spoon mixture into a greased and lined 10" cake tin.
6 Bake in a pre-heated oven 170°C/325°F/Gas 3 for 2-2 $^1/_2$ hours.
   (Variations: For 1 pt water, use $^3/_4$ pt water and $^1/_4$ pt orange juice.
   For dried fruit, use 8 oz fruit and 2 ripe mashed bananas or 1 large grated
   cooking apple).

Mary Christie, Bon Accord, Aberdeen

Bijou Cake

8 oz (225g) S. R. flour

$^1/_2$ tsp cinnamon

a pinch of salt

4 oz (100g) butter

8 oz (225g) currants

8 oz (225g) raisins

4 oz (100g) mixed peel

2 oz (50g) soft brown sugar

a few chopped almonds (optional)

1 egg, beaten

1 dsp syrup

$^1/_2$ tsp bicarbonate of soda

$^1/_4$ pt (150ml) milk

Method:

1 Mix flour with cinnamon and salt.
2 Rub in butter and add currants, raisins, peel, sugar and almonds.
3 Beat egg with syrup, then add to dry ingredients and mix well.
4 Dissolve soda in milk and mix well into the mixture.
5 Spoon mixture into a greased and lined deep 7" cake tin.
6 Bake in a pre-heated oven 180°C/350°F/Gas 4 for 45 minutes, then reduce to
   160°C/325°F/Gas 3 for 1 $^3/_4$ hours.
   (Note: This cake can be used as a Christmas cake.)

Elizabeth Montgomery, St. Vincent St. - Milton, Glasgow

Rich Fruit Cake

4 oz (100g) butter
4 oz (100g) caster sugar
4 eggs, well beaten
8 oz (225g) plain flour
^{1}/4 tsp baking powder

6 oz (175g) sultanas (or mix
 with raisins)
6 oz (175g) currants
4 oz (100g) cherries, quartered
4 oz (100g) walnuts, chopped

Method:

1 Cream butter and sugar.
2 Add eggs alternately with flour and baking powder.
3 Stir in fruit and nuts and mix well together.
4 Spoon mixture into a greased and lined 8" tin.
5 Bake in a pre-heated oven 160°C/325°F/Gas 3 for 2 hours.
   (Note: This cake makes a lovely Christmas cake when covered with marzipan and
      Royal icing and can be darkened by using dark brown sugar in place of
      caster sugar.
      Double quantities for cake takes 3-3 ^{1}/4 hours to bake.)

C. E. Rose, Greyfriars, Inverness

Bride's Cake

12 oz (350g) butter or margarine
12 oz (350g) soft brown sugar
6 eggs, beaten
2 tblsp treacle
1 lb (450g) plain flour
1 tsp almond essence
2 tblsp coffee (made)
1 tsp mixed spice
1 tsp cinnamon

2 oz (50g) whole almonds
2 oz (50g) ground almonds
grated rind of 1 orange
12 oz (350g) currants
8 oz (225g) raisins
1 lb (450g) sultanas
4 oz (100g) cherries
2 oz (50g) mixed peel
2 oz (50g) preserved ginger

Method:

1 Cream butter and sugar, add eggs with a little flour and treacle.
2 Add flour, essence, coffee, spice, cinnamon, both almonds and rind.
3 Mix in dried fruit, cherries, peel and ginger and mix well.
4 Spoon mixture into a deep lined tin.
5 Bake in a pre-heated oven 160°C/325°F/Gas 3 for 3 hours.

J.C. Bain, Killearnan

Small Cakes, Tarts & Biscuits

Queen Cakes

4 oz (100g) margarine
4 oz (100g) caster sugar
2 eggs

6 oz (175g) S. R. flour
1 tsp baking powder

Method:

1 Cream margarine and sugar and mix in one egg with some flour.
2 Add second egg, remainder of flour and baking powder and beat well.
3 Put spoonfuls of mixture into paper cake cases.
4 Bake in a pre-heated oven 200°C/400°F/Gas 6 for 10-15 minutes.

Hughina Gunn, Skerray

Raisin Buns

4 oz (100g) margarine
4 oz (100g) soft brown sugar
2 eggs, beaten

4 oz (100g) S. R. flour
4 tblsp All-Bran, crushed
4 oz (100g) raisins

Method:

1 Cream margarine and sugar, then add eggs and flour.
2 Add bran and raisins and mix well.
3 Put spoonfuls of mixture into paper cake cases.
4 Bake in a pre-heated oven 190°C/375°F/Gas 5 for 15-20 minutes.

Joan Macleod, Cross, Lewis

Nutty Meringues

2 egg whites
1 cup caster sugar

1 cup Rice Krispies
2 cups Cornflakes, crushed

Method:

1 Beat egg whites until stiff.
2 Add half the sugar and beat until smooth.
3 Fold in remaining sugar, Rice Krispies and Cornflakes.
4 Place spoonfuls of mixture on bakewell paper or greased sheet.
5 Bake on lowest shelf of a pre-heated oven 140°C/275°F/Gas 1 for 1 hour.
   (Variation: When cold, base of meringue may be dipped in melted chocolate).

May Keith, Ayr

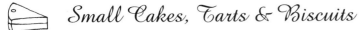

Coconut Tartlets

Shortcrust Pastry:
4 oz (100g) plain flour
$^1/_2$ tsp baking powder
a pinch of salt
3 oz (75g) margarine
1 egg yolk, beaten in a little cold water
raspberry jam

Filling:
1 egg white
$^1/_2$ cup coconut
$^1/_2$ cup sugar
a pinch of salt

Method:

1   To make pastry, sieve the dry ingredients together in a bowl.
2   Rub in margarine and mix to a stiff dough with egg and water.
3   Knead dough, roll out pastry and use to line patty tins.
4   Put a $^1/_4$ tsp of jam in each pastry case.
5   Beat egg white until very stiff.
6   Add other filling ingredients and mix well.
7   Put a small spoonful of mixture over jam in each pastry case.
8   Bake in a pre-heated oven 190°C/375°F/Gas 5 for approx. 20-25 minutes
until risen and set.

A. Mackenzie, Ballyclare E.P.C., N. Ireland

Butter Tartlets

6 oz (175g) shortcrust pastry (see Coconut Tartlets)
Filling:
1 oz (25g) butter
4 oz (100g) demerara sugar
1 egg, beaten

4 oz (100g) currants
a few drops vanilla essence
glacé icing
cherries

Method:

1   Roll out pastry thinly, cut into 3" rounds and use to line patty tins.
2   Melt butter, add remaining ingredients and mix well.
3   Put a small spoonful of mixture into each case.
4   Bake in a pre-heated oven 200°C/400°F/Gas 6 for 15-20 minutes.
5   Cover with a little glacé icing and decorate with cherries.

Sheila Macdonald, Lochcarron

Cherry Franzipan

Shortcrust Pastry:

6 oz (175g) plain flour

3 oz (75g) soft margarine

1 oz (25g) caster sugar

1 egg

Method:

1　Mix all ingredients together with a fork to form a firm dough.
2　Knead lightly, roll out and use to line an 8" flan ring.

Filling:

4 oz (100g) margarine

4 oz (100g) caster sugar

3 oz (75g) semolina

1 egg

2 oz (50g) cherries

4 oz (100g) marzipan

3 oz (75g) raisins

icing sugar

Method:

1　Beat margarine, sugar, semolina and egg together until smooth and creamy.
2　Chop cherries and marzipan and add with raisins to mixture.
3　Spread mixture into prepared pastry case.
4　Bake in a pre-heated oven 180°C/350°F/Gas 4 for 35-40 minutes.
5　Sprinkle with icing sugar when cold and cut into wedges.

Ruth MacDonald, Greyfriars, Inverness

Almond Tart

Shortcrust pastry (see Cherry Franzipan)

apricot jam

Filling:

4 oz (100g) ground almonds

2 large eggs, beaten

2 cups caster sugar

2 tsp almond essence

Method:

1　Line 8" flan tin with pastry and spread with jam.
2　Mix together all ingredients (except $^1/_4$ cup sugar).
3　Spread mixture into prepared pastry case and sprinkle with remaining sugar.
4　Bake in a pre-heated oven 160°C/325°F/Gas 3 until golden brown.

M. Macleod, Barvas, Lewis

 *Tarts*

Border Tart

Shortcrust pastry (see Cherry Franzipan)

Filling:

2 oz (50g) margarine
3 oz (75g) caster sugar
1 egg, beaten
1 cup mixed fruit

few drops vanilla essence
pinch of baking powder
glacé icing to decorate

Method:

1 Line a 7" flan tin with pastry.
2 Cream margarine and sugar and beat in egg.
3 Stir in remaining ingredients and mix well.
4 Spoon mixture into prepared pastry case.
5 Bake in a pre-heated oven 230°C/450°F/Gas 8 for 5 minutes then reduce heat to 200°C/400°F/Gas 6 for 20 minutes.
6 Dribble glacé icing onto cooled tart.

Rene Stewart, St Columba, Edinburgh

Bakewell Tart

Shortcrust pastry (see Cherry Franzipan)
jam

Filling:

4 oz (100g) margarine
4 oz (100g) caster sugar
2 eggs, beaten

1/2 tsp almond essence
2 oz (50g) S. R. flour
2 oz (50g) cake crumbs

Method:

1 Line two 7" flan tins with pastry and spread with jam.
2 Cream margarine and sugar and add eggs with essence.
3 Add sifted flour and crumbs and spread mixture over jam.
4 Bake in a pre-heated oven 180°C/350°F/Gas 4 for 35-40 minutes.
5 May be eaten hot or cold. If cold, cover with glacé icing.

Nora Cook, Knockbain

Shortbread (1)

8 oz (225g) butter
3 oz (75g) caster sugar
3 oz (75g) ground rice or Farola

3 oz (75g) cornflour
6 oz (175g) plain flour

Method:

1 Melt butter in pan and gradually add dry ingredients.
2 Press mixture into a Swiss roll tin.
3 Bake in a pre-heated oven 190°C/375°F/Gas 5 for 25 minutes.
4 Cut into fingers while hot and sprinkle with caster sugar.

Anne Hamilton, Cumbernauld

Shortbread (2)

1 cup S. R. flour
2 cups plain flour
1 cup caster sugar

1 cup cornflour
8 oz (225g) butter

Method:

1 Mix all dry ingredients together in a bowl.
2 Melt butter slowly, pour into dry mixture and knead lightly.
3 Press mixture into 2 greased 7" sandwich tins.
4 Bake in a pre-heated oven 160°C/325°F/Gas 3 for 1 hour.
5 Cut into wedges while hot and sprinkle with caster sugar.

Nan Macaulay, Drumchapel, Glasgow

Shortbread (3)

8 oz (225g) butter
5 oz (150g) caster sugar
2 oz (50g) Farola

2 oz (50g) cornflour
10 oz (225g) plain flour

Method:

1 Cream butter and sugar together and add Farola and cornflour.
2 Add plain flour one spoonful at a time and knead gently.
3 Press mixture onto a floured surface and cut into squares.
4 Transfer squares onto a baking tray.
5 Bake in a pre-heated oven 130°C/260°F/Gas ³/4 for 15 minutes then reduce heat to
   110°C/225°F/Gas ¹/4 for 45-50 minutes. (Do not allow to brown).

Katie MacPherson, Portree, Skye

Shortbread & Biscuits

Demerara Shortbread

8 oz (225g) butter
4 oz (100g) icing sugar

8 oz (225g) S. R. flour
4 oz (100g) cornflour
demerara sugar

Method:

1. Cream butter and icing sugar and add flour and cornflour.
2. Divide into 4 sausage shapes and roll in demerara sugar.
3. Cut into slices and lay, well apart, on a greased baking tray.
4. Bake in a pre-heated oven 180°C/350°F/Gas 4 for 20-25 minutes.

Amy Maclean, Kyle

Flakemeal Shortbread

4 oz (100g) margarine
4 oz (100g) porridge oats
1 level tsp baking powder

2 1/2 oz (65g) S. R. flour
2 oz (50g) demerara sugar

Method:

1. Melt margarine, stir in all other ingredients and mix well.
2. Press mixture into a greased Swiss roll tin.
3. Bake in a pre-heated oven 180°C/350°F/Gas 4 for 30-40 minutes.
4. Cut carefully into squares, cool and sprinkle with caster sugar.

Gillian Conolly, Knock E.P.C., N. Ireland

Coconut Biscuits

4 oz (100g) margarine
4 oz (100g) caster sugar

4 oz (100g) S. R. flour
4 oz (100g) coconut
a pinch of salt

Method:

1. Cream margarine and sugar.
2. Gradually work in dry ingredients to make a stiff dough.
3. Either roll dough out and cut with a cutter, or form into a sausage shape and cut into slices.
4. Place, well spaced out, on a baking tray.
5. Bake in a pre-heated oven 180°C/350°F/Gas 4 for 15-20 minutes.

Elma MacKenzie, Lochinver

Empire Biscuits (1)

8 oz (225g) soft margarine
2 oz (50g) icing sugar
8 oz (225g) plain flour

Method:

1 Cream margarine and sugar and mix in flour.
2 Knead together and chill dough for $^1/_2$ an hour.
3 Roll out to $^1/_4$" thickness, cut into rounds and place on a baking tray.
4 Bake in a pre-heated oven 190°C/375°F/Gas 5 for 8-10 minutes.
5 Sandwich together with jam, cover with glacé icing and decorate with a halved cherry.

R. McNicol, Dumbarton

Empire Biscuits (2)

6 oz (175g) margarine
2 oz (50g) icing sugar

6 oz (175g) plain flour
2 tblsp custard powder

Method:

1 Cream margarine and sugar lightly, add flour and custard powder and mix well together.
2 Roll out thinly, cut into rounds and place on a baking tray.
3 Bake in a pre-heated oven 180°C/350°F/Gas 4 for 10 minutes.
4 Sandwich together with jam, cover with glacé icing and decorate with a cherry.
   (Note: Empire biscuits keep best when stored in an airtight tin and sandwiched and iced only when required.)

C. J. Sinclair, Dingwall

Custard Creams

Method:

1 Use same ingredients as for previous recipe and mix well.
2 Roll into small balls, flatten and mark with a fork dipped in flour and place on a baking tray.
3 Bake in a pre-heated oven 180°C/350°F/Gas 4 for 20 minutes.
4 Cool on a wired tray and sandwich together with butter icing.

Butter Icing:

Cream together -
2 oz (50g) butter or margarine
4 oz (100g) icing sugar

Pat MacDonald, Bracadale, Skye

Peanut Buttons

5 oz (150g) peanut butter
4 oz (100g) white vegetable fat
4 oz (100g) caster sugar
4 oz (100g) light brown sugar
9 oz (250g) plain flour
1 tsp bicarbonate of soda
$^1/_2$ tsp salt

1 egg, beaten
2 tblsp milk
1 tsp vanilla essence
caster sugar for tossing
chocolate buttons

Method:

1　Cream peanut butter, fat and sugars together.
2　Add dry ingredients, egg, milk and essence and mix well to form a stiff dough.
3　Roll into small balls and toss in caster sugar.
4　Place 2" apart on a greased baking tray.
5　Bake in a pre-heated oven 190°C/375°F/Gas 5 for 10 minutes.
6　Top each cookie immediately with a chocolate button, pressing down so that the cookie cracks around the edges.

Sadie Lane, Coatbridge

Ginger Oaties

8 oz (225g) margarine
1 level tblsp syrup
1 tsp bicarbonate of soda, dissolved
　in 1 tblsp boiling water

2 cups sugar
2 cups S. R. flour
2 cups porridge oats
2 tsp ginger (optional)

Method:

1　Melt margarine and syrup and stir in all other ingredients.
2　Place in heaps on a greased baking tray.
3　Bake in a pre-heated oven 180°C/350°F/Gas 4 for 15 minutes.

Helen MacDonald, Elgin

Muesli Biscuits

4 oz (100g) butter
6 oz (175g) soft brown sugar
1 egg, beaten
$^1/_2$ tsp vanilla essence

6 oz (175g) plain flour
$^1/_2$ tsp bicarbonate of soda
6 oz (175g) muesli
a pinch of salt

Method:

1　Cream butter and sugar until light and fluffy.
2　Beat in egg with essence and add all other ingredients.
3　Place heaped teaspoonfuls of mixture on a greased baking tray and flatten with a fork.
4　Bake in a pre-heated oven 180°C/350°F/Gas 4 for 10-15 minutes.
5　Leave for 2 minutes before removing to cool on a wire tray.

E. Thomson, Tain

Snicker Doodles

11 oz (300g) caster sugar
2 tsp cinnamon
4 oz (100g) soft margarine
4 oz (100g) Cookeen
1 tsp vanilla essence
2 eggs, beaten

12 oz (350g) S. R. flour
2 level tsp cream of tartar
1 level tsp bicarbonate of soda
$^1/_2$ tsp salt

Method:

1 Mix 2 tblsp caster sugar with 2 tsp cinnamon in a saucer.
2 Cream remaining caster sugar, margarine, Cookeen and essence.
3 Add eggs and mix in flour, cream of tartar, bicarbonate of soda and salt.
4 Roll mixture into small balls (1" diameter) and toss in caster sugar and cinnamon.
5 Place about 2" apart on a greased baking sheet.
6 Bake in a pre-heated oven 200°C/400°F/Gas 6 for 8-10 minutes.
    (Note: This quantity makes 7-8 dozen light and crispy biscuits. They keep very well in
        an airtight tin.)

Christine Davidson, Watten

Melting Moments

3 oz (75g) butter
3 oz (75g) cooking fat
5 oz (150g) caster sugar
1 egg, beaten
10 oz (275g) S. R. flour
1 tsp vanilla essence

crushed cornflakes
cherries for decorating

Method:

1 Cream butter, fat and sugar together.
2 Add egg, flour and vanilla essence and mix well.
3 Roll into small balls and cover in cornflakes.
4 Place on a baking tray and press $^1/_4$ cherry on top.
5 Bake in a pre-heated oven 180°C/350°F/Gas 4 for 15-20 minutes.

S. Brown, Stranmillis E.P.C., N. Ireland

Oat Biscuits

4 oz (100g) margarine
3 oz (75g) sugar
6 oz (175g) oatflakes
2 oz (50g) plain flour

Method:

1 Cream margarine and sugar and add oats and flour.
2 Knead together and roll out into a square.
3 Cut into fingers or rounds and place on a baking tray.
4 Bake in a pre-heated oven 180°C/350°F/Gas 4 for 15-20 minutes.

J. Bell, Dornoch

Traybakes & Truffles

Florentine Fingers

Base:

6 oz (175g) plain flour
3 oz (75g) butter/margarine
1 1/2 oz (40g) icing sugar

Topping:

3 3/4 oz (90g) margarine
4 oz (100g) caster sugar
1 oz (25g) sultanas
2 oz (50g) walnuts, chopped
2 oz (50g) cherries, chopped
1 tblsp cream (or top of milk)

Method:

1 Mix base ingredients together to stiff consistency.
2 Press into a greased 11" x 7" Swiss roll tin.
3 Bake in a pre-heated oven 180°C/350°F/Gas 4 for 15-20 minutes until pale golden.
4 Melt margarine and sugar, boil for 1 minute, stirring all the time.
5 Stir in fruit and nuts, add cream and spread over shortcake base.
6 Bake in a pre-heated oven 160°C/325°F/Gas 3 for 10-15 minutes.
7 Mark fingers while hot and allow to cool in tin.
8 Dip ends in melted chocolate when cold.

Mairi Ferguson, Aultbea

Toffee Tart- Millionaire's Shortcake

Base:

4 oz (100g) margarine
2 oz (50g) caster sugar
6 oz (175g) plain flour

Topping:

4 oz (100g) margarine
4 oz (100g) caster sugar
4 tsp syrup
1 small tin condensed milk
4 oz (100g) chocolate, melted

Method:

1 For base, cream margarine and sugar and gradually add flour.
2 Press mixture gently into an 11" x 7" Swiss roll tin.
3 Bake in a pre-heated oven 180°C/350°F/Gas 4 for 20 minutes.
4 Put topping ingredients (except chocolate) into pan and bring slowly to the boil.
5 Boil for 3-4 minutes, stirring all the time.
6 Remove from heat, beat for 3 minutes and pour over cold base.
7 Leave to set and cover caramel with chocolate when cold.
8 Cut into squares or fingers when set.

Millie Morrison, Carloway, Lewis

Orange Cake

8 oz (225g) butter or margarine	14 oz (400g) wholemeal flour
1/2 pt (300ml) fresh orange juice	2 tsp baking powder
10 oz (275g) demerara sugar	6 tblsp icing sugar
2 eggs beaten	3 tblsp orange juice

Method:

1 Melt margarine, add all other ingredients (except icing sugar and juice) and beat well.
2 Pour into a greased deep baking tray approx. 7" x 10".
3 Bake in a pre-heated oven 180°C/350°F/Gas 4 for 60-70 minutes.
4 Mix icing sugar and orange juice, pour over hot cake and cut into squares when cold.

Mina Fraser, Kyle

Ginger Iced Oatcake

4 oz (100g) margarine	**Topping:**
2 level tblsp syrup	6 level tblsp icing sugar
4 oz (100g) soft brown sugar	3 oz (75g) butter
8 oz (225g) rolled oats	1 level tsp ground ginger
2 level tsp ground ginger	3 level tsp syrup
a little melted fat	

Method:

1 Melt margarine and syrup in a pan over gentle heat and mix in dry ingredients.
2 Press into a Swiss roll tin, brushed with melted fat, and level with a knife.
3 Bake in a pre-heated oven 180°C/350°F/Gas 4 for 20-25 minutes.
4 Put all topping ingredients into a pan and melt over gentle heat.
5 Pour over oatcake and cut into squares when cold.

Anne Snoddy, Lairg

Eilidh's Munchies

8 oz (225g) milk cooking chocolate	4 oz (100g) coconut
1 egg	4 oz (100g) glacé
4 oz (100g) caster sugar	cherries or walnuts

Method:

1 Melt chocolate, pour into a greased 11" x 7" Swiss roll tin and leave to set.
2 Beat egg and sugar together, add coconut and cherries or walnuts and spread mixture over firm chocolate.
3 Bake in a pre-heated oven 180°C/350°F/Gas 4 for 20 minutes.
4 Cut into squares when cold.

Helen Smith, Resolis

 *Traybakes*

Fruit Squares

6 oz (175g) brown sugar
4 oz (100g) rolled oats
6 oz (175g) plain flour
$^1/2$ tsp salt

6 oz (175g) butter
10 oz (275g) mincemeat
1 egg, beaten

Method:

1   Combine sugar, oats, flour and salt and mix well.
2   Rub in butter until mixture resembles coarse crumbs.
3   Spread half the mixture into an 11" x 7" Swiss roll tin and cover with mincemeat.
4   Spread remaining crumb mixture over fruit and gently brush with egg.
5   Bake in a pre-heated oven 200°C/400°F/Gas 6 for 20-25 minutes.
6   Cut into bars when cold.

Valerie MacDonald, Carloway, Lewis

Mincemeat Squares

Shortcrust Pastry:

8 oz (225g) plain flour
4 oz (100g) margarine

Filling:

jam
mincemeat
3 egg whites
3 oz (75g) caster sugar
3 oz (75g) ground almonds

Method:

1   Knead pastry ingredients and press into a 11" x 7" Swiss roll tin.
2   Spread jam over pastry and cover with mincemeat.
3   Whisk egg whites until stiff, fold in sugar and almonds and spread over mincemeat.
4   Bake in a pre-heated oven 180°C/350°F/Gas 4 for 35-45 minutes.
5   Dust with caster sugar and cut while hot.

Minnie Macleod, Stoer

Walnut Fruit Fingers

6 oz (175g) butter
6 oz (175g) brown sugar
4 oz (100g) S. R. flour
2 oz (50g) walnuts, chopped
4 oz (100g) sultanas or raisins

2 oz (50g) medium oatmeal
1 egg
1 tsp vanilla essence
chocolate glacé icing

Method:

1   Melt butter, cooking until slightly syrupy, and mix in all other ingredients.
2   Press into a greased 11" x 7" Swiss roll tin.
3   Bake in a pre-heated oven 180°C/350°F/Gas 4 for approx 20 minutes.
4   Cover with icing while hot.
5   Leave to cool in tin and cut into fingers.

Chrissy McInnes, Greenock

Honey Date Bars

3 oz (75g) plain flour
1 tsp baking powder
pinch of salt
4 oz (100g) dates, chopped
2 oz (50g) nuts

2 eggs, beaten
4 tblsp honey
2 oz (50g) butter, melted

Method:

1 Sieve dry ingredients together and mix with dates and nuts.
2 Blend together eggs, honey and butter, add to dry ingredients and mix well.
3 Press into a greased 8" square tray.
4 Bake in a pre-heated oven 180°C/350°F/Gas 4 for 25 minutes.

Rena MacKay, St. Vincent St.-Milton, Glasgow

Bridal Slices

5 oz (150g) shortcrust pastry (see Mincemeat Squares)
2 oz (50g) margarine
4 oz (100g) caster sugar
8 oz (225g) raisins or sultanas
4 oz (100g) cherries, chopped
6 digestive biscuits, crushed

1 tsp mixed spice
2 eggs, beaten
a little jam
marzipan
thick glacé icing

Method:

1 Cream margarine and sugar, add fruit, cherries, biscuits and spice.
2 Bind together with beaten eggs.
3 Roll out pastry and use to line an 11" x 7" Swiss roll tin.
4 Spread jam over pastry and cover with fruit mixture.
5 Bake in a pre-heated oven 180°C/350°F/Gas 4 for 45 minutes.
6 Leave to cool, cover with a layer of marzipan and top with glacé icing.

Peggy MacDonald, Partick Highland, Glasgow

Coconut Ice Squares

8 oz (225g) margarine
4 dsp caster sugar

2 cups plain flour
2 cups cornflakes
1 1/2 cups coconut

Method:

1 Melt margarine and mix well with dry ingredients in a bowl.
2 Press into a greased 11" x 7" Swiss roll tin.
3 Bake in a pre-heated oven 180°C/350°F/Gas 4 for 20-25 minutes.
4 Ice while warm, using icing sugar, boiling water and a drop of vanilla essence.
5 Cut into fingers or squares when cool.

E. Thomson, Tain

 *Traybakes*

Brownies

2 eggs
7 oz (200g) caster sugar
4 oz (100g) plain chocolate,
   broken in pieces

4 oz (100g) butter or margarine
7 oz (200g) plain flour
1 1/2 tsp baking powder
4 oz (100g) walnuts, chopped

Method:

1   Whisk eggs and sugar together until light and fluffy.
2   Melt chocolate and butter in a bowl over a pan of hot water.
3   Stir into the egg mixture, then add flour, baking powder and nuts.
4   Spread into a greased 11" x 7" Swiss roll tin.
5   Bake in a pre-heated oven 180°C/350°F/Gas 4 for 30-35 minutes or until crust has formed.

I. More, Burghead

Streusel Squares

6 oz (175g) caster sugar
3 oz (75g) margarine
1 egg, beaten
a pinch of salt
6 oz (175g) S. R. flour
1/4 pt (150ml) milk

Topping:

1 oz (25g) margarine, melted
3 oz (75g) soft brown sugar
2 oz (50g) walnuts, chopped
1 tsp cinnamon
1 oz (25g) S. R. flour

Method:

1   Cream sugar and margarine until fluffy, add egg and beat well.
2   Sieve salt and flour into creamed mixture with the milk and mix.
3   To make topping, mix margarine and sugar, add walnuts, cinnamon and flour.
4   Spoon half of the cake mixture into a greased 11" x 7" tin and sprinkle with half the topping.
5   Cover with remaining cake mixture and sprinkle on rest of topping.
6   Bake in a pre-heated oven 180°C/350°F/Gas 4 for 35-40 minutes.
7   Cut into squares when cold.

Jessie Bray, Greenock

Praline Squares

4 oz (100g) margarine
4 oz (100g) caster sugar
2 oz (50g) S. R. flour
2 oz (50g) coconut
2 oz (50g) cooking chocolate, grated

2 oz (50g) ground almonds
2 eggs, beaten
3 drops almond essence
chocolate for covering

Method:

1   Cream margarine and sugar.
2   Add all dry ingredients, eggs and essence.
3   Press into a lined 11" x 7" Swiss roll tin.
4   Bake in a pre-heated oven 180°C/350°F/Gas 4 for 20-25 minutes.
5   Cover with melted chocolate when cold and cut into squares.

Peggy Ross, Fearn

Flapjacks

4 oz (100g) margarine
4 oz (100g) brown sugar

3 oz (75g) syrup
8 oz (225g) rolled oats

Method:

1 Melt margarine, sugar and syrup in a pan over a slow heat.
2 Stir in oats and mix well.
3 Press mixture into a greased 11" x 7" Swiss roll tin.
4 Bake in a pre-heated oven 180°C/350°F/Gas 4 for 25–30 minutes.
5 Cut into fingers while still warm.

M. Lockerby, Lochs, Lewis

Fruit and Nut Flapjacks

5 oz (150g) soft margarine
3 oz (75g) soft brown sugar
5 oz (150g) golden syrup

10 oz (275g) muesli
4 oz (100g) porridge oats
1 tblsp orange juice

Method:

1 Melt margarine, sugar and syrup together.
2 Mix in muesli, oats and juice.
3 Spread mixture into an 11" x 7" Swiss roll tin.
4 Bake in a pre-heated oven 190°C/375°F/Gas 5 for 35-40 minutes until golden brown.
5 Cut flapjacks with sharp knife when cold.

N. Ross, Fearn

Crunchies

6 oz (175g) margarine
4 oz (100g) sugar
1 tblsp syrup

5 oz (150g) rolled oats
2 oz (50g) Rice Krispies
1 oz (25g) chopped nuts
1 tsp bicarbonate of soda

Method:

1 Melt margarine, sugar and syrup in a pan.
2 Stir in dry ingredients.
3 Press mixture into an 11"x7" Swiss roll tin.
4 Bake in a pre-heated oven 180°C/350°F/Gas 4 for 20 minutes.
5 Mark while warm and cut into squares when cold.

Elizabeth MacKay, Buccleuch & Greyfriars, Edinburgh

 *Traybakes*

Canadian Roll

13 digestive biscuits, crushed
13 marshmallows, snipped

13 cherries, chopped
1 small tin condensed milk
coconut

Method:

1   Mix all ingredients together, make into a sausage shape and roll in coconut.
2   Put in fridge to set and then cut into slices.
     (Variation: Add 1 tblsp coconut to mixture and press into a Swiss roll tin.
         Cover with chocolate and cut into squares when set.)

Dolly MacKenzie, East Kilbride

Marshmallow Squares

3 oz (75g) butter
9 oz (250g) marshmallows
1 tblsp orange juice

2 oz (50g) raisins
grated rind of 1 orange
6 oz (175g) Rice Krispies

Method:

1   Melt butter in a large pan over a low heat.
2   Add marshmallows and orange juice and stir until marshmallows are melted.
3   Remove from heat, add raisins, rind and Rice Krispies and mix well.
4   Press mixture into a greased and lined Swiss roll tin.
5   Leave to chill for 30 minutes and cut into squares.

K. MacLean, Sleat, Skye

Toffee Crisp

1 bag marshmallows (approx. 200g)
2 bars Highland toffee
4 oz (100g) margarine
6-7 oz (175-200g) Rice Krispies
icing sugar

Method:

1   Melt marshmallows, toffee and margarine in a large pan.
2   Remove from heat and add Rice Krispies.
3   Press mixture into a lined Swiss roll tin.
4   Dust with icing sugar, allow to set and cut into bars.

Annabel Robertson, Dundee

Ginger Squares

4 oz (100g) margarine
1 small tin condensed milk
2 tblsp syrup
3 oz (75g) caster sugar

8 oz (225g) ginger nut
   biscuits, crushed
1 tsp ground ginger
5 oz (150g) cooking chocolate, melted

Method:

1 Put margarine, milk, syrup and sugar in a pan.
2 Bring to boil and simmer for 8 minutes.
3 Remove from heat, add biscuits and ginger and mix well.
4 Press into a Swiss roll tin and cover with melted chocolate.
5 Cut into small squares when set.

L. McKnight, Elder Memorial, Leith

Iced Lemon Squares

8 oz (225g) margarine
8 oz (225g) white cooking chocolate
2 tblsp syrup
12 oz (350g) "Nice" biscuits, crushed
4 oz (100g) coconut

Icing:

icing sugar
juice and rind of 1 lemon
lemon colouring
a little coconut

Method:

1 Melt margarine, chocolate and syrup in a pan.
2 Add biscuits and coconut and mix well.
3 Press mixture into a Swiss roll tin.
4 Make glacé icing with icing sugar, lemon juice and colouring.
5 Cover mixture with icing and sprinkle with extra coconut.
5 Cut into squares when set.

Fiona Morrison, St. Vincent St. -Milton, Glasgow

Fudge Slices

4 oz (100g) margarine
6 oz (175g) sugar
1 small tin condensed milk
2 tblsp syrup

8 oz (225g) digestive
   biscuits, crushed
1-1 1/4 tblsp cocoa, or
   drinking chocolate
5 oz (150g) cooking chocolate, melted

Method:

1 Melt margarine, sugar, milk and syrup over a low heat.
2 Add dry ingredients and press mixture into a Swiss roll tin.
3 Cover with melted chocolate and cut into slices when set.

Grace Wylie, Oban

Date Tray Bake

8 oz (225g) margarine
1 small cup sugar
8 oz (225g) dates, finely chopped

1 egg, beaten
vanilla essence
10 oz (275g) tea biscuits, crushed

Method:

1. Melt margarine, sugar and dates in a pan.
2. Allow to cool and add egg and essence.
3. Bring to boil, then remove from heat and mix in biscuits.
4. Press mixture into a Swiss roll tin.
5. Sprinkle with caster sugar when cold and cut into squares.

Mary Sutherland, Urray

Traybake

4 oz (100g) butter
4 oz (100g) plain chocolate
4 oz (100g) seedless raisins

1 small tin condensed milk
8 oz (225g) digestive
   biscuits, crushed

Method:

1. Melt butter and chocolate in a pan over a low heat.
2. Remove from heat, stir in raisins and add milk and biscuits.
3. Press mixture into a greased Swiss roll tin and coat with melted chocolate if desired.

Anne MacKenzie, Grant St., Glasgow

Crispie

4 Mars Bars, sliced
4 oz (100g) butter
4 oz (100g) Rice Krispies
6 oz (175g) cooking chocolate (optional)

Method:

1. Melt Mars Bars and butter in a large pan over a low heat.
2. Remove from heat and mix in Rice Krispies.
3. Press into a Swiss roll tin and put in fridge to set.
4. Cover with melted chocolate, allow to set and cut into bars.

R. MacLeod, Bracadale, Skye

Fruit and Nut Bars

3 Snickers Bars
3 oz (75g) block margarine
3 oz (75g) Rice Krispies
2 oz (50g) raisins
6 oz (175g) cooking chocolate

Method:

1   Melt Snickers Bars and margarine in a large pan over a low heat.
2   Remove from heat and mix in Rice Krispies and raisins.
3   Press into a Swiss roll tin and put in fridge to set.
4   Cover with melted chocolate, allow to set and cut into bars.

Dolina Guthrie, Point, Lewis

Bounties

8 oz (225g) coconut
1 small tin condensed milk

2 oz (50g) icing sugar
cooking chocolate

Method:

1   Put coconut, milk and sugar into bowl and mix thoroughly.
2   Roll mixture into balls (rub hands with icing sugar to prevent sticking) and flatten slightly.
3   Dip each bounty into melted chocolate, using a skewer.
4   Place on greaseproof paper and allow to set.

Margaret Gilmour, Fort Augustus

Coffee Kisses

4 oz (100g) butter
8 oz (225g) icing sugar
6 oz (175g) coconut
2 oz (50g) walnuts, crushed

1 tblsp Camp coffee essence
cooking chocolate

Method:

1   Cream butter and sugar and add coconut and walnuts.
2   Beat well and add coffee essence.
3   Roll mixture into balls and chill for 1 hour.
4   Dip balls, using a skewer, into melted chocolate to cover.

M. Macleod, Lochs, Lewis

 *Truffles*

Peanut Butter Balls

8 oz (225g) jar peanut butter
1 ¹/2 cups cornflakes, crushed
1 cup icing sugar

1 oz (25g) soft margarine
12 oz (350g) milk cooking chocolate
walnuts for decoration

Method:

1   Put peanut butter, cornflakes, sugar and margarine in a bowl and mix thoroughly.
2   Roll mixture into balls of the required size and chill.
3   Dip balls, using a skewer, into melted chocolate to cover.
4   Decorate with a walnut.

Marion Miller, Fortrose

Truffles

1 large tin condensed milk
4 oz (100g) margarine
20 digestive biscuits, crushed

4 tblsp coconut
2 tblsp drinking chocolate
coconut or vermicelli

Method:

1   Melt milk and margarine over a low heat.
2   Add biscuits, coconut and chocolate and mix well.
3   Roll mixture into balls (dampen hands to prevent sticking).
4   Dip into coconut or vermicelli.

Mary Black, Rosskeen

Chocolate Macaroons

4 oz (100g) margarine
8 oz (225g) sugar
4 oz (100g) drinking chocolate

4 tblsp milk
8 oz (225g) porridge oats
8 oz (225g) coconut

Method:

1   Melt margarine and sugar over a low heat.
2   Add chocolate and milk and simmer for a few minutes.
3   Remove from heat and stir in oats and coconut.
4   Roll mixture into balls and cover in coconut.

M. Munro, Snizort, Skye

Preserves and Chutneys

CHUTNEY

Gooseberry and Lemon Jam

2 large lemons, rind grated, pith removed and discarded.
2 1/2 lb (1.25 kg) gooseberries, washed, topped and tailed
1 pt (600 ml) water
3 lb (1.5 kg) granulated or preserving sugar, warmed

Method:

1 Chop lemons roughly, reserving juice and tying pips in a small piece of muslin cloth.
2 Put gooseberries, water, lemon rind, pulp, juice and pips in a large pan.
3 Bring to the boil, cover and simmer for 30 minutes, stirring frequently.
4 Discard muslin bag, gradually add sugar, stirring gently over a low heat until dissolved.
5 Boil until setting point. (When a teaspoonful on a saucer wrinkles when pushed with the finger).
6 Remove from heat, skim surface and leave aside for 10 minutes.
7 Pour into warmed jars, cover and label.

Minnie MacLeod, Greenock

Strawberry Jam

2 lb (1 kg) strawberries
3 lb (1.5 kg) caster sugar
juice of 2 medium lemons

Method:

1 Put ingredients into a large pan and bring slowly to the boil.
2 Continue to boil until fruit is tender.
3 Cool, and, when ready for pouring, stir steadily for 5 minutes to ensure that the berries are well mixed through the jam.
4 Pour into jars, cover and label.

A. and C. Calder, Glenshiel

Lemon Cheese

4 oz (100g) butter
1 lb (450g) sugar

grated rind and juice of
3 lemons
6 eggs, well beaten

Method:

1 Beat butter and sugar well in front of fire (or in mixer!).
2 When soft add rind and juice of lemons and mix thoroughly and add eggs.
3 Stir cheese over a low heat until it is thick and creamy, but do not let it boil.
4 Pour into jars when cold, cover and label.

Margaret MacKay, Carloway, Lewis

119

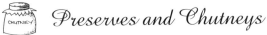

Marmalade (1)

1 lb (450g) marmalade oranges
1 sweet orange
1 lemon

10 cups water
5 lb (2.25 kg) sugar

Method:

1 Cut up fruit and put pips into a bowl with 1 cup water.
2 Mince or liquidise fruit, add remaining water and leave overnight.
3 Add strained liquid from pips and sugar, bring to boil and boil for 40 minutes.
4 Test for setting and remove from heat when ready.
5 Stir, pour into warmed jars, cover and label.

Elizabeth Campbell, Duirinish, Skye

Marmalade (2)

2 grapefruit, minced
2 lemons, minced
2 oranges, minced

5 pt (2.5 litre) water
small knob of butter
8 lb (3.5 kg) sugar

Method:

1 Put juice, fruit, and pips (tied in a muslin bag) in preserving pan with water and leave for 24 hours.
2 Bring to the boil and boil until fruit is soft and pulpy.
3 Add butter to help remove scum.
4 Warm sugar and add to mixture in pan.
5 Boil until setting point is reached.
6 Pour into warmed jars, cover and label.

L. McKnight, Elder Memorial, Leith

Busy Housewife's Grapefruit Marmalade

4 grapefruit, quartered
2 lemons, quartered

2 pt (1120 ml) water
7 ^{1}/$_2$ lb (3.4 kg) sugar

Method:

1 Put fruit (without pips) and water in a pressure cooker.
2 Cook at full pressure (15 lbs) for 12-15 minutes.
3 Remove from heat until pressure falls to normal (10 minutes).
4 Liquidise, or process, fruit to reduce skins to desired size.
5 Return to pan, add sugar and heat slowly to dissolve sugar.
6 Bring to boil, stirring constantly and boil for 5-10 minutes.
7 Pour immediately into hot jars, cover and label.
   (Note: There is no need for the muslin bag of pips as the pectin rich pith is included. This gives a sure quick set marmalade.)

I. MacPherson, Dornoch

Rowan and Apple Jelly

3 lb (1.5 kg) rowan berries

3 lb (1.5 kg) apples

water

sugar (1 lb (450g)
   to each pint juice)

Method:

1   Put rowans in a pan with just enough water to cover berries and cook slowly until pulpy.
2   Repeat the procedure with the apples.
3   Strain both fruits through a jelly bag and add sugar to mixed juices.
4   Boil rapidly for 20-30 minutes until setting point.
5   Pour into jars, cover and label.

Irene Chisholm, Inverasdale

Green Tomato Chutney

5 lb (2.25 kg) green tomatoes, sliced

1 lb (450g) onions, chopped

$^{1}/_{2}$ oz (15g) peppercorns

1 oz (25g) salt

1 lb (450g) sugar

2 pt (1 litre) vinegar

8 oz (225g) raisins

8 oz (225g) sultanas

Method:

1   Mix tomatoes, onions, peppercorns and salt and leave for 24 hours.
2   Put sugar, vinegar, raisins and sultanas in a pan, bring to the boil and simmer for 5 minutes.
3   Add the tomato and onion mixture and simmer until thick.
4   Pour into jars, cover when cold and label.

Georgie MacLeod, Stoer

Uncooked Chutney

1 lb (450g) dates

1 lb (450g) sultanas

1 lb (450g) apples

1 lb (450g) onions

1 lb (450g) demerara sugar

1 pt (600ml) vinegar

1 tsp salt

1 tsp pepper

1 tsp cayenne pepper

1 tsp ginger

Method:

1   Mince dates, sultanas, apples and onions.
2   Add remaining ingredients and stir well.
3   Leave for 24 hours, stirring occasionally.
4   Pour into jars, cover and label.

D. MacEwan, Free North, Inverness

Apple Chutney

4 lb (1.8 kg) apples,
  peeled and cored
1 lb (425g) sultanas
8 oz (225g) onions

grated rind and juice
  of 1 lemon
1 dsp ground ginger
1 1/2 pt (900ml) vinegar
2 lb (900g) soft brown sugar

Method:

1 Mince apples, sultanas and onions and put in a pan.
2 Add rind and juice of lemon, ginger and 1 pt (600ml) vinegar.
3 Dissolve sugar in remaining vinegar and add to mixture.
4 Cook until chutney is thick.
5 Pour into warm jars, cover when cold and label.

I. MacLeod, Lochs, Lewis

Rhubarb Chutney

10 cups rhubarb, sliced
1 pt (600ml) vinegar
1 onion, finely chopped
4 lb (1.8 kg) sugar
1/4 tsp salt

1 tblsp ground ginger
2 tblsp cinnamon
1 tsp mixed spice
1 tsp ground cloves

Method:

1 Simmer rhubarb in vinegar until tender.
2 Add onion, sugar, salt and spices.
3 Cook slowly until mixture thickens, stirring frequently.
4 Cool, pour into jars, cover and label.

Mary Smith, Drumchapel, Glasgow

Beetroot Chutney

3 lb (1.5 kg) beetroot
2 large onions
1 1/2 lb (675g) apples, peeled and cored
8 oz (225g) demerara sugar

1 tsp ground ginger
juice of 1 lemon
1 pt (600ml) vinegar
1 level tblsp salt

Method:

1 Boil beetroot for approx. 1 1/2 hours, cool and peel.
2 Mince beetroot with onions and apples.
3 Put mixture into a large pan and add all other ingredients.
4 Boil until soft, stirring frequently.
5 Cool, pour into jars, cover and label.

Catherine MacKenzie, Assynt

Miscellaneous

Fried Rolled Oats

Heat a good quantity of cooking oil in frying pan up to chip heat. Add sufficient rolled oats to take up the oil, keeping up the heat and stirring vigorously to prevent sticking. Add a little salt and a fair amount of black pepper. When oat flakes have begun to turn brown, remove from heat but continue to stir for a few minutes longer. Do not leave on low heat. Can be served with hot mushrooms, fried or scrambled eggs, or cold as a relish with a meat or fish dish or practically anything savoury.

Elizabeth MacKay, Buccleuch & Greyfriars, Edinburgh

Crowdie

Heat 2 pints of milk slightly (approx. 72°F). Stir in ¹/₂ pint rennet. Allow mixture to set. Cut into cubes and leave until whey rises to the top. Pour off whey through muslin. Tie up curds in muslin and hang for an hour or two to drain. Break up with fingers and salt to taste.
Eat with oatcakes.
(Note: The whey makes good oatcakes without the addition of fat.)

J. M. Morrison, Carloway, Lewis

"Highland Haggis"

12 oz (350g) cream cheese
6 oz (175g) cheddar cheese, grated
1 tblsp onion, finely chopped
1 tblsp green pepper, finely chopped
pinch of salt
pinch of cayenne pepper
walnuts, finely chopped

Method:

1   Combine the two cheeses and mix in all the other ingredients.
2   Shape into a roll and leave in fridge for 1 hour.
3   Roll in chopped walnuts.
4   Serve with Ritz crackers 1 hour after removing from fridge.

Muriel Amey, Helmsdale

 *Miscellaneous*

Cheese and Onion Puffs

1 packet of puff pastry
4 oz (100g) cheddar cheese, grated
1 medium onion, grated

1 egg, beaten
$^1/_2$ tsp dry mustard
pinch of salt and pepper

Method:

1 Roll out pastry and cut with cutter to appropriate size for patty tins, making bases and lids.
2 Mix all other ingredients together.
3 Place spoonfuls of mixture into pastry-lined tins, top with lids and seal.
4 Bake in a pre-heated oven 200°C/400°F/Gas 6 for 15-20 minutes.

Grace Irvine, Ayr

Cheese and Chive Hotties

1 fresh medium white sliced loaf
soft butter or margarine
8 oz (225g) cheddar cheese, grated
chives, chopped
salt and pepper

melted butter
paprika

Method:

1 Remove crusts and butter the required slices of bread.
2 Sprinkle each slice with cheese, chives and seasoning.
3 Roll up each slice from the shorter edge, wrap each roll in greaseproof paper and chill.
4 Remove the paper and arrange rolls on baking trays.
5 Brush with melted butter and dust with paprika.
6 Bake in a pre-heated oven 230°C/450°F/Gas 8 for 5-10 minutes.

Isobel Cresswell, Ayr

Apple and Raisin Sauce

1 lb (450g) cooking apples
1 oz (25g) sugar
1 tblsp raisins
1 tblsp cinnamon
1 tblsp lemon juice

Method:

1 Peel apples and chop roughly.
2 Put into a pan with all the other ingredients.
3 Simmer until apples are soft.
4 Serve with pork.

Marietta MacDonald, Carloway, Lewis

Plum Pudding and Dumpling Sauce

2 eggs, separated
2 oz (50g) butter
1 cup caster sugar
2 tblsp apple juice or cider
$^1/_2$ cup rich milk or cream

Method:

1 Beat egg whites and set aside.
2 In top of double boiler, cream butter and sugar.
3 Add juice (or cider) and the well-beaten egg yolks.
4 Mix well and stir in the milk or cream.
5 Cook in double boiler until it is as thick as custard.
6 Pour the mixture gradually into the beaten egg whites, beating all the time.
7 Serve warm or chilled with pudding or dumpling.

Margaret MacKay, Toronto, Canada

Leny's Warm Raisin Sauce

1 pt (600ml) tea
8 oz (225g) raisins
4 tblsp syrup (from stem ginger)
1 tblsp lemon juice
1 tsp cinnamon
cornflour to thicken
sugar to taste

Method:

1 Make tea with tea-bags and simmer raisins in this for 1 hour.
2 Remove tea-bags and add syrup, lemon juice and cinnamon.
3 Thicken with cornflour and add sugar to taste.
4 Serve hot or cold over ice-cream.

Fiona Morrison, St Vincent St.-Milton, Glasgow

Microwave Chocolate Sauce

2 oz (50g) plain chocolate

1-2 oz (25-50g) caster sugar

1 knob butter

2 fl oz water

Method:

1 Melt chocolate for 1 ¹/₂ minutes on "High"
2 Add sugar, butter and water.
3 Microwave 1 minute on "High" until butter melts.
4 Beat until smooth.

Miriam Thompson, Knock E.P.C., N. Ireland

Microwave Fudge

12 oz (350g) cooking chocolate

1 small tin condensed milk

1 oz (25g) margarine

4 oz (100g) walnuts

Method:

1 Put all ingredients in a suitable bowl.
2 Microwave for 3 minutes, remove and stir well.
3 Spread in a greased Swiss roll tin and cut into squares when set.

Catherine Fraser, Kyle

Treacle Toffee

1 lb (450g) brown sugar

1 small tin condensed milk

2 tblsp treacle

6 oz (175g) butter

2 tblsp syrup

Method:

1 Melt all ingredients in pan and bring slowly to the boil.
2 Boil carefully for 30 minutes.
3 Pour into oiled tin and cut into squares when set.

Mary Ross, Tain

Helensburgh Toffee

4 oz (100g) butter

1 cup milk

2 lb sugar

1 large tin condensed milk

¹/₄ bottle vanilla essence

Method:

1 Melt butter in pan with cup of milk.
2 Add sugar and when dissolved boil for 5 minutes, stirring all the time.
3 Add condensed milk and boil for 20 minutes.
4 Remove from heat and allow to settle before adding essence.
5 Beat until forming grains.
6 Pour into greased tray and cut into squares when set.

Isbbel Campbell, Lochgilphead

Fresh Tomato Juice

2 lb (900g) ripe tomatoes, chopped
1 tsp soft brown sugar
4 tblsp lemon juice
2 drops tabasco
^{1}/2 tsp salt
Worcester sauce to taste
strip of lemon peel

Method:

1 Place all ingredients (except lemon peel) in liquidiser.
2 Blend at high speed until tomatoes are thoroughly pulped.
3 Sieve to remove pips and pieces of skin.
4 Place the strip of lemon peel in the juice.
5 Cover and refrigerate for a minimum of 1 hour to allow the flavour of the lemon peel
   to infuse.
6 Serve in glasses, garnished with a slice of cucumber.

Janet Morrison, Stoer

Lemonade

4 lemons (or oranges)
2 ^{1}/4 lb (1 kilo) sugar
^{1}/2 oz (15g) Epsom salts
^{1}/2 oz (15g) citric acid   } *available at chemists*
^{1}/2 oz (15g) tartaric acid
2 ^{1}/2 pt boiling water

Method:

1 Grate and squeeze lemons.
2 Put rind, juice, sugar, Epsom salts, citric and tartaric acids in a large bowl and add the
   boiling water.
3 Stir until all the ingredients have dissolved.
4 Leave to cool and strain into clean bottles.
5 Dilute to taste.

Elizabeth Finlayson, Castletown

 *Miscellaneous*

Elder Flower Wine

2 lemons
8 pt water
1 ¹/4 lb (550g) sugar
7 elder flower heads
2 tblsp wine or white vinegar

Method:

1 Squeeze lemons, retaining juice and peel.
2 Boil water and pour over sugar, stirring until dissolved.
3 When cold put in flower heads, juice and rind of lemons and vinegar.
4 Stand for 24 hours, strain and bottle in screw-top bottles.

Anon, Nairn, Croy & Ardersier

An Excellent Pick-Me-Up!

10 eggs, plus shells
6 lemons
8 oz (225g) demerara sugar
2 large cartons fresh cream
¹/2 bottle Orange Grove Rum

Method:

1 Break eggs with shells into a large bowl.
2 Add juice of lemons.
3 Soak for 4 days!
4 Sieve.
5 Add remaining ingredients.
6 Bottle.

Peggy Morrison, Kinloch, Lewis

Lus-Na-Laogh

Take about 20 stems of "Pink Saxifrage" flowers, found at the edge of fresh water lochs.
Clean them thoroughly and cut them up into small sizes.
Boil them for 12 hours in 6 pints of water.
Dispose of stems and sieve water twice through a clean cloth.
Bottle, ready to drink a small glass every day until the carbuncle disappears!

B. MacDonald, Lochs, Lewis